THREE LETTERS TO THE DUKE OF WELLINGTON

THREE

LETTERS

TO THE

Duke of Wellington

BY

THE EARL OF LAUDERDALE

[1829]

REPRINTS OF ECONOMIC CLASSICS

Augustus M. Kelley, Bookseller
New York 1965

Library of Congress Catalogue Card Number
64 - 7668

THREE LETTERS

TO THE

DUKE OF WELLINGTON.

THREE LETTERS

TO THE

DUKE OF WELLINGTON,

ON THE

FOURTH REPORT OF THE SELECT COMMITTEE OF
THE HOUSE OF COMMONS,

APPOINTED IN 1828 TO ENQUIRE INTO THE PUBLIC INCOME
AND EXPENDITURE OF THE UNITED KINGDOM;

IN WHICH THE

NATURE AND TENDENCY OF A SINKING FUND
IS INVESTIGATED,

AND THE

FALLACY OF THE REASONING BY WHICH IT HAS BEEN
RECOMMENDED TO PUBLIC FAVOUR IS EXPLAINED.

BY

THE EARL OF LAUDERDALE.

———

LONDON:
JOHN MURRAY, ALBEMARLE STREET.

1829.

CONTENTS.

LETTER I.

*Displays the inconsistency betwixt the principles laid
down by the Committee to guide Parliament on the
subject of a Sinking Fund, and the measures they have
recommended to be pursued.*

MY DEAR DUKE,

I CONFESS I am one of those who never expected
much benefit from the appointment of the Committee
of Finance, on whom the task was imposed, in the
last Session of Parliament, of examining into and of
reporting upon the present state of the revenue and
expenditure of the United Kingdoms, as well as
that of suggesting the system most expedient to be
pursued in the future management of what is denominated our national debt.

To me that measure always appeared to be an un-
constitutional delegation of the duties of the Chancellor of the Exchequer to a Committee of the House
of Commons, pregnant with evil to the best interests of
the community ; for though the character and reputation to be acquired by suggesting plans, from which
great public benefit may in future arise, is perhaps
the strongest excitement to exertions of individual

industry, it loses its efficacy when the fame to be gained is to be shared out amongst many.

Besides, when plans are to be framed by the united efforts of a numerous Committee, experience precludes our expecting anything but the hesitating recommendation of feeble measures, arising out of a compromise of conflicting opinions; often mischievous, and always unaccountable, unless to those who were present at the various controversies out of which they originated.

Neither did this appear to me to be the sole, or even the greatest source of injury which the public had to dread, from such a trust being reposed in a Committee of the House of Commons; for it seemed obvious that, if the leading Members of that House were to be made joint participators in the formation of plans subsequently to be submitted to Parliament, the efficacy of that check and controul which, for the benefit of the people, is wisely lodged by the constitution in the hands of their representatives, could not fail to be impaired; for a man must be ignorant of human nature, who does not know that the partiality with which authors naturally view their own works, and the feelings of lenient indulgence with which they are disposed to comment upon them, must destroy that rigid and scrupulous examination of the measures submitted to Parliament, which the people have a right to expect from their representatives.

Though, for these reasons it was, from the first, impossible for me to approve of the arrangement, or to form any sanguine expectation of benefit from the result of the labours of this Committee, I certainly did not at the time feel, and do not now mean, in the most distant manner to insinuate, that the Government over which you so deservedly preside, did wrong in sanctioning the appointment.

They were called to the management of public affairs, at a time when the universal expectation of the community was wound up prophetically to attribute to such an appointment future solid advantages, most important to the welfare of the nation. It had been held forth as the great boon the country was to derive from what, during the indecorous flirtation that preceded the unprincipled union with the powerful party with which he connected himself, was designated the master mind of Mr Canning, our late minister. And the persuasion of great and important benefits to be derived from it, must, in public estimation, have acquired increased vigour from the circumstance of its being generally believed that a dispute about the composition of this intended Committee had induced those, in whom His Majesty, subsequent to Mr Canning's death, had reposed his confidence, to withdraw from offices, the attainment of which, it is the vulgar prejudice to believe is the sole object of every man who takes part in political controversy.

Far, therefore, from censuring the share you had in the appointment, I am disposed to maintain that the Government, in whom His Majesty, fortunately for the country, now reposes his confidence, acted wisely in persevering in the long projected experiment; and it is impossible that the impartiality displayed in selecting the Committee, which secured the aid and assistance of men of all parties and connections, without any apparent desire of establishing a preponderating influence in its deliberations, should not command universal approbation.

When the result of the labours of the Committee thus constituted were first brought under the consideration of Parliament, indisposition had compelled me to desist attending my duty, and I derived the first intelligence of the contents of the Fourth Report, from learning that you, in the House of Lords, had concurred with Lord Bexley in declaring that it contained more important information than any Report that had ever been made to Parliament, and that you had expressed a sanguine hope that the statement therein made, together with the discussions it had occasioned and might produce, would put an end to all the fallacies now prevalent, and convince Parliament and the country, that the salvation of the state depends upon keeping up an efficient Sinking Fund.

It is now upwards of twenty-four years, since I submitted to the public my reasons for thinking,—in the first place, that the Sinking Fund, as established by Mr Pitt, in 1786, (a measure perfectly similar in principle to that adopted by Sir Robert Walpole, in 1717), was delusive, elusory, and fallacious ;—and, in the second place, that all sinking funds, proceeding on the principle of giving an artificial direction to a portion of the wealth of a community by forcibly converting an arbitrary amount of its revenue into capital, must be prejudicial to the increase of public wealth, and detrimental to the welfare of every country that resorted to such means of attempting to discharge, what is vulgarly and ignorantly called its public debt.

Since that period, I have had many powerful co-adjutors in establishing the first of those propositions; and, though I have not had the same powerful assistance in relation to the second, I cannot charge my recollection with ever having seen any attempt to invalidate the doctrine, from which I then inferred, that parsimony, or abstracting from expenditure in consumable commodities, forcibly to convert a portion of the revenue of a country into capital, impeded the natural progress by which public wealth increases, and was injurious to every community who improvidently adopted such a practice.

The subject, indeed, has never since, for any great length of time, been absent from my mind, and, from a careful and attentive observation of all that has passed, I am now, more than ever, confirmed in a thorough belief of the soundness of the opinion I then delivered : subsequent reflection has only induced me to think that I did not push my conclusions to the extent that in reason they ought to have been carried ; and, with this impression on my mind, you cannot be surprised when I say, that I differ with you to such an extent, that, instead of conceiving an efficient Sinking Fund necessary for the salvation of the state, I hesitate not to announce a distinct opinion, that such an institution, under the present state of the distribution of property in this country, is, of all others, calculated to produce the greatest injury to the public. And, whilst on this, the most essential of all points in relation to our finance, I am unfortunately constrained to hold an opinion so much at variance with that which you at present entertain, I am afraid I differ more widely on the merits of the Report you have thought yourself justified in praising.

For to me, it appears that, in regard to the future arrangements to be adopted in the management of the Sinking Fund, on the supposition that it is to be continued, the only general principles this Committee lay down as essential, are so completely at variance with the measures they recommend for the regulation of the conduct of Parliament, that, if a Chancellor of the Exchequer had, in the form of a speech in the House of Commons, uttered the substance of their Report, the public censure he must have incurred would have been ruinous to his character as a Minister; but, what is still more material, I must think that the great and important question as to the expediency of continuing the establishment of a sinking fund, is treated in a manner so superficial, and with a poverty of thought so disgraceful, that, though the Members of that Committee have somehow been induced to submit it as the production of their united efforts, it is impossible for me, who have long admired the talents of many of those who compose it, and who know them all, to believe that there is a man among them who would not have been ashamed to have submitted it to the public as a production of his own.

In support of the first of these propositions, I will, in this letter, after transcribing in a note that part of the Report which relates to the Sinking Fund, give a short statement of the principles, which the Committee seem to have laid down as incontrovertible; and, by comparing them with the measure they have recommended, and which Parliament, with the concurrence of Government, has since adopted, I feel confident the inconsistency must be rendered so apparent, as to make it difficult for any one to persevere in expressing approbation of the Report.

With regard to the more important question of the expediency of persevering to provide for a sinking fund in the present situation of the country, as this measure has long been regarded with almost universal favour, both on account of its supposed efficacy in reducing what is called our national debt, and on account of the power attributed to it of increasing our public wealth, it is my intention to address to you two other letters.

In the first of these, I mean to assign my reasons for thinking that the grounds are completely fallacious, on which both the friends and the foes of this institution have uniformly argued, from the time of Mr Hutchinson, the great supporter, and, I believe, the original projector of Sir Robert Walpole's Sinking Fund, down to the last Session of Parliament, when the Report was made, which you have honoured with your approbation ; and, upon what I think a more accurate view of the situation of a country, which, for a great length of time, has had recourse to the funding system to raise the means of defraying its extra expenditure, and which, in vulgar language, is said to be deeply involved in debt ; to found an argument, the object of which will be to prove, that the establishment of a sinking fund, instead of alleviating, is the means, of all others the most efficacious, in aggravating the sole evil, which such a state of its affairs can inflict on any community.

And, in the second of these letters, I will endeavour to satisfy you and the public, that the measure of funding, by which a community acquires the means of defraying a greater extra expenditure, than it could otherwise command for immediate use, instead of impoverishing, has had, and always must have, the effect of increasing the public wealth of every country where the practice is resorted to ; and further, that the system of compulsive parsimony, which a sinking fund always establishes, and on which it alone can proceed, instead of tending to increase public wealth, is of all others the device that must most rapidly impoverish any community, who improvidently has recourse to it.

I will not be guilty of the folly of attempting to anticipate what will be the effect of my views of this subject either on your mind or that of the public ; but, as an apology for once more renewing my efforts, allow me to say that I feel perfectly confident I will leave no doubt in the mind of any man of the inconsistency that pervades the Report of the Committee in respect of the principles they have laid down, and the measures they have recommended; and that I undertake the farther task of satisfying you and the public, that a sinking fund must aggravate the sole evil which a public debt inflicts on a community, as well as that of proving that it must diminish the public wealth of the country in which it is established, with a sanguine hope that my efforts will be more efficacious than they have heretofore been.

For I conceive there are points of view, in which this question has not hitherto been regarded, that tend to relieve the mind from the load of prejudice naturally arising out of our usual style of expressing ourselves, and the consequent prevalent mode of contemplating the subject, which must give rise to doubt and hesitation in the minds of those who have habitually cherished the opinion, that extra expenditure diminishes the collective wealth of the community; and, when a doubt is once raised of the rectitude of that train of reasoning, which has so universally prevailed, I am sanguine in thinking that a conviction of the fallacy of the conclusions to which it leads must speedily ensue.

Besides, it is impossible not to perceive, that the public mind is better prepared to receive just impressions on the merits of an institution, of which there universally existed enthusiastic admiration at the time I at first attempted to open the eyes of the community to the mischiefs it would inflict. I must also add, that my hopes of success are increased, because I know the powerful aid I should acquire, if I could make an impression on the mind of the man entrusted by his Majesty with the important office you now hold; and because, without intending any compliment, I have no difficulty in saying that you are, in my estimation, the person who has held that office, during my long existence in public life, least likely to be swayed by the ridiculous boast of maintaining uniformity of opinion, and most certain, exclusively to pride yourself in boldly adopting that line of conduct, which in your conscience you conceive most advantageous for the country.*

That the few short observations I am to make on the inconsistency of the Report may be more distinctly followed, and, if erroneous, more easily checked, I think it right to subjoin, in a note, that part of it which relates to the future establishment of our Sinking Fund, and which, as it has exclusively commanded Lord Bexley's admiration and your praise, is the only part of the Report on which it is my intention to make any observation.†

---

* This was written long before you had given to the world that splendid illustration of its truth, which your conduct on the Catholic question has afforded.

† " Having stated the progress made in the diminution of the public debt since the close of the late war, it remains for the Committee to express their opinion with respect to the measures to be adopted prospectively for the further accomplishment of the same object.

Now, waiving for the present all consideration of the question how far it is expedient to keep up a Sinking Fund, or, as the Committee express it, "how

---

" They have already stated, that they could not, under any circumstances, recommend a system involving the principle of raising funds for the extinction of debt, by the creation of it in another shape.

" The Committee is impressed with a strong conviction of the sound policy of applying a surplus revenue perseveringly in those times during which no extraordinary resources need be raised, in the reduction of the debts accumulated to defray the expenses of antecedent periods of difficulty and exertion. Without offering at present any opinion on the comparative advantages of defraying the charges of war, by the immediate imposition of taxes, to the amount of those charges, or by raising the required supplies by loans, the Committee consider that, if a nation has been induced, for the sake of greater present facilities and safety, to provide for such exigencies by a system of borrowing, whereby a permanent annual charge has been created, that nation is bound, on the return of peace, to make every effort, consistent with a due regard to the other burthens upon the people, for the reduction of that charge. A course of policy founded upon the avowed principle of raising loans for the exigences of the state in time of war, and of making no provision for diminishing the permanent charge of those loans in time of peace, must appear an abandonment of all consideration for the credit and safety of the country, in the eventual occurrence of future difficulties and dangers.

" If the accumulated debt of each period of extraordinary exertion is to be handed down undiminished, as a load upon those who are thereafter to meet the exigences of other struggles and other difficulties, it is too obvious to require an argument, that the time cannot be very distant (according to the ordinary vicissitudes of peace and war, in the history of human affairs) when the combined weight of the past and present burthens must become too great

" far it is sound policy to apply a surplus revenue
" perseveringly, in those times during which no extra-
" ordinary sources need be raised for (what they are

---

for the most prosperous people to support, and the fabric of public
credit must crumble under the accumulated pressure.

" The system of borrowing during the war, and gradually redeem-
ing the debt, thereby created, during peace, is an intermediate
course between the resolute exertion of raising at once, by taxes,
the whole of the supplies required, and the easier plan of providing for the existing difficulty by the easiest present means, without
regard to the interests or safety of future generations.

" Impressed with these sentiments, the Committee would have
recommended a perseverance in the resolution of Parliament in
1819, to apply 5,000,000l. annually, to the gradual extinction of
debt, if that measure could have been accomplished by the application of a surplus revenue, and without the necessity of borrowing,
or of adding new burthens upon the country.

" But as it is obvious from what they have submitted to the
House, that there is at present no clear surplus to that amount,
nor any immediate prospect of such a surplus arising; and as it
is also clear that since the year 1822, Parliament has not thought
it expedient to make provision for such a surplus (except by the
nominal aid of the sale of the half-pay annuity); the Committee
are of opinion, that, instead of a fixed Sinking Fund, the real surplus of revenue only should be appropriated annually, in the mode
hereafter stated, to the reduction of debt

" Although the future surplus which would result from the
estimate formed by the Committee, cannot be reckoned upon as
amounting to more than 2,000,000l., applicable to the payment of
the Life Annuities now charged on the Sinking Fund, and the
further reduction of debt, they are not without the hope, that by
some reduction of expense which may be effected, and by some
augmentations which may be obtained by regulations and modifica-

" pleased to call) the reduction of the debts accumu-
" lated to defray the expenses of antecedent periods of
" difficulty and of danger," which will subsequently

---

tions of the revenue, without new taxes, that surplus may in future years be raised to the amount of 3,000,000*l.*

" The Committee, upon the whole, are of opinion, that the following principle, in the future regulation of the Sinking Fund, should be adopted :—That, regard being had to the total amount and fluctuating nature of our revenue, as well as to the necessity not only of carefully avoiding any addition to the public debt, but also of reducing it as far as possible in time of peace, it will be expedient, in estimating the Supply and Ways and Means, to keep in view the necessity of a surplus of not less than 3,000,000*l.* in each year, but that in case the eventual annual surplus should not amount to 3,000,000*l.* the deficiency ought not to be supplied by borrowing.

" They are also of opinion, that all funded debt redeemed by the application of the real surplus of revenue should be cancelled.

" In recommending the application, upon this principle, of the real surplus revenue to the reduction of the public debt, the Committee have in view the employment of that surplus in the extinction of the unfunded, as well as in the redemption of the funded debt, and notwithstanding the present high price of Exchequer Bills, and consequently light charge to the public, of the debt outstanding upon these securities, yet considering the embarrassment and loss which, under certain contingencies, might arise from the existence of a large debt payable on demand, the Committee are of opinion, that the policy of effecting a gradual reduction of the unfunded debt should not be lost sight of.

" The Committee are also of opinion, that in the employment of the surplus revenue in the reduction of the debt, some advantage might be obtained by the application of it to the conversion of permanent into temporary annuities, to whatever extent parties be taken into consideration; it appears that the Committee, have stated three leading principles as governing their opinion on the future regulation of that Sinking Fund they deem it expedient to maintain.

1st. They have declared " that they could not, " under any circumstances, recommend a system in- " volving the principle of raising funds for the extinc- " tion of debt by the creation of it in another shape."

2ndly. They have given a distinct opinion, "that, " instead of a fixed Sinking Fund, the real surplus of " revenue should only be, in future, annually appro- " priated to the reduction of debts."

3rdly. They have decidedly stated, " that all

---

holding the former might be disposed to effect the change upon equitable terms for the public.

" A computation will be found in the Appendix to this Report, showing to what extent such a conversion might be effected with a given amount of sinking fund, under various suppositions, with respect to the prices of stocks, &c.

" As it might, however, require more time than the present state of the Session would conveniently afford, to prepare a Bill for effecting any material alteration in the details of the Sinking Fund, it would, perhaps, be most advisable, to pass an Act forthwith (if the House should concur in opinion with the Committee) for enabling the Commissioners for the reduc- tion of the national debt to diminish the application of the funds now placed by law at their disposal from the present amount to a fund, at the rate of 3,000,000*l.* a year, including the dividends on the stock already redeemed, and standing in their name; a measure which the Committee conceive would be, under existing circumstances, the best preliminary to the introduction of a final arrangement of this very important subject in the next Session of Parliament."

" funded debt in future redeemed by the application
" of the real surplus of revenue should be cancelled."

Having laid down these principles as the premises
on which their reasoning was to proceed, it was
certainly to have been expected, that the measure
recommended to Parliament, would have been such
as naturally flowed from the principles they had
thus adopted ; it cannot, however, be denied that,
with a perfect disregard to all these rules for guid-
ing their own conduct and that of Parliament, which
they had thus deliberately announced; they conclude
by recommending " that an Act should be passed,
" enabling the Commissioners for the reduction of
" the National Debt, forthwith to diminish the appli-
" cation of the funds now placed by law at their
" disposal, from the present amount of five millions
" to a fund at the rate of three millions a year,
" including the dividends on the stock already
" redeemed, and standing in their name."

To establish the gross inconsistency which this
recommendation involves, requires (as the Committee say) no argument. It is impossible for any
one, however captious, to dispute that this measure,
which they have submitted for the immediate adop-
tion of Parliament, is in violation of every principle
to which they had antecedently acceded, as fitting
to govern the decision of Parliament.

1st. As they had declared " that the future surplus
" could not be reckoned upon as amounting to more
" than two millions applicable to the life annuities,
" now charged on the Sinking Fund, and to the fur-

B

" ther reduction of the debt," it follows that three millions cannot be so applied, without raising funds for the extinction of debt by the creation of debt in another shape ; a proceeding they had just stated, they could, under no possible circumstances, recommend.

2ndly. Though, without reserve, they had declared their opinion " that instead of a Sinking Fund " to a fixed amount, the surplus of revenue only " should be appropriated annually to the reduction of " debt," they nevertheless recommend to Parliament to persevere in a fixed Sinking Fund, and that to an amount greater than any surplus they anticipate.

3rdly. Though they formally announce that, in their opinion, " all the debt in future to be redeemed " by the real surplus of the revenue should be cancelled," this arrangement particularly specifies the dividends on the stock already redeemed as forming a component part of this proposed Sinking Fund.

It is true, that this plan is recommended only for the present year, as preliminary to the introduction of some final arrangement; but this was not what the public had been taught to expect; they had been flattered with the hope that the profound investigation by the Committee of the important question, so interesting to the community, and of late so much agitated, would have enabled the House permanently to decide upon what was most expedient for the interests of the country. Indeed, it was with this view of the duty to be imposed on them, clearly and distinctly expressed, that Mr Canning, after admitting the habits of his life had never led him to a minute and deliberate consideration of the subject, originally proposed the appointment of this Committee. It is impossible, therefore, that the public should not be disappointed, when they learn that the boasted efforts, from which so much was expected, have ended in the recommendation of a temporary measure, in itself directly contradictory to every opinion contained in this Report, which by some has been strangely regarded as the most valuable financial document ever submitted to Parliament.

Besides, it is certain, that, though they have decidedly declared an efficient Sinking Fund to be necessary for the welfare of the State, stating that, without such an establishment, the fabric of public credit must crumble under the pressure of past and future burdens, they have nevertheless furnished Parliament with no distinct plan for any future permanent arrangement. On the contrary, the few vague suggestions they have submitted on the subject are distinguished by the same wavering inconsistency that is displayed in regard to the temporary measure they have definitively recommended.

After stating their conviction of the necessity of maintaining a Sinking Fund, they distinctly declare that they would have wished to persevere in the resolution adopted by Parliament in the year 1819, of applying five millions annually to the extinction of our debt, " if that measure could have been " accomplished by the application of a surplus of

" revenue, and without the necessity of borrowing
" or of adding new burdens upon the country."

But, as it was obvious, from the statement they
had submitted to Parliament, that there neither was
at that time any such clear surplus, nor any immediate prospect of its arising, they announced a
definitive opinion that in future the real surplus of
revenue should be annually appropriated for this
purpose, and that in a mode, which they promised
to state in a future part of the Report.

It seems, however, most extraordinary that, when
they come to give to the House a direct statement
of the principle that should guide the future regulation of the fluctuating Sinking Fund arising out of
the real surplus of revenue, their instructions terminate in a recommendation to keep in view the
necessity of a Sinking Fund to the amount of the
fixed sum of three millions annually ; and for this
three reasons are specifically stated, each of which
must appear to the common understanding of mankind to authorise a very opposite conclusion.

1st. They announce the necessity of having regard to the total amount and the fluctuating nature
of our revenue, in itself a natural preamble to any
suggestion concerning the mode of applying the
actual surplus of the revenue ; but certainly a very
extraordinary one to the instruction, which immediately follows, to keep in view the necessity of a
surplus in each year to the fixed amount of three
millions.

2ndly. The same observation applies to the

pointed direction concerning the necessity of care-fully avoiding any addition to the public debt; for, without disregarding the caution, it must have appeared to those from whom it proceeded; that in enjoining the Parliament to keep in view the neces-sity of a surplus of three millions, they recom-mended them prospectively to look to a very distant event, if no loan was to be contracted for that purpose; as in the antecedent paragraph, they had stated their opinion of the impossibility of reckoning on a surplus of more than two millions, applicable to the payment of life annuities, as well as the further reduction of the debt; and they express only a dis-tant hope that, through the medium of laying increased burdens on the people, by means of regulations and modifications of the revenue, it might in future years be raised to three millions.

Lastly, In pressing with urgency the duty of hav-ing regard to the necessity of reducing the debt as far as possible, in time of peace, they have neverthe-less limited the view they recommend to be taken, to the necessity of a surplus of three millions, whilst they specially guard against the eventual surplus being increased by borrowing, or by the applica-tion of the income arising from a redeemed debt; and, as they had previously protested against new taxes as a means of increasing the surplus, it follows that the only source of augmentation was to be derived from regulation and modification in the mode of collecting the existing taxes, which, whatever the Committee may think, is just as fertile a source of increasing the burdens of the people, as if a new tax were imposed; as it is the amount of the sum levied, and not the nature of the tax, or the date at which it is imposed, that is really burdensome to those that are subjected to it.

But it would be endless to persevere in commenting on the disgusting inconsistency exhibited in that part of the Report, which, assuming the expediency and even the necessity of a Sinking Fund, treats of the arrangements to be pursued, either in the temporary or in the future management of that establishment; for the Committee can be justified by no man, who attentively considers the principles they have laid down, which, almost in every instance, would lead to the approbation of measures directly opposite to those subsequently recommended.

Such a Report may indeed command the admiration of Lord Bexley, as forming a fit associate for the resolution which he recommended to Parliament, at a time when the Notes of the Bank of England were exchanging for less than fifteen shillings, which, if I recollect right, declared " that the Pro- " missory Notes of the Bank of England have hitherto " been, and are at this time, held to be equivalent to " the legal coin of the realm, in all pecuniary trans- " actions to which such coin is legally applicable;" or for that, which equally emanated from him, which attributed to the Crown the power of *altering and varying the value*, as well as that of regulating the weight and fineness of our coin,—a power which certainly could not be exercised, without regulating the price of every commodity, and affixing a maximum to each.

But it is to the multiplicity of business pressing upon you at the moment, which left no time for consideration of its contents, to which I can alone attribute your joining in the praise of this Report; for, though the Committee have collectively brought it forward, I am convinced there is not one of the intelligent members who formed it would have risked his character by adopting it as his own, or who could now conscientiously join in the panegyric Lord Bexley has pronounced on it.

In truth, the variations of sentiment, which the absence of some and the presence of others must from day to day create in the prevalent opinion of a numerous Committee, of whom a majority are to decide, as well as the compromise of conflicting opinions, and the evil which the necessity of making a Report always inflicts, ought to have led all who had had experience of what has heretofore taken place, or who possess power of reasoning on the probable consequences of the measure, to anticipate the result, and should have dissuaded both Government and Parliament from resorting to such an arrangement.

On this branch of the subject, however, I will make no further observation; indeed the seeming applause which you expressed of the Report is the only apology I can offer for having gone so much into detail; for, whether it is consistent or inconsistent in the regulations it has recommended for the future management of a Sinking Fund, becomes immaterial, if, as I anticipate, it can be established beyond a doubt, that a Sinking Fund is the means of all others the most efficacious of aggravating the sole evil, which (what is called) a great public debt inflicts; and that it is the measure of all others that must most rapidly impoverish any community who imprudently resort to it.

Yours, &c. &c. &c.

LAUDERDALE.

LETTER II.

Explains the fallacy of the reasoning, by which the establishment of a Sinking Fund has hitherto been recommended to public favour; and contends—First, that the sole evil inflicted on a community, by loans and funding, as a means of providing for extra expenditure, arises from the great and sudden alteration it produces in the distribution of property—Secondly, that a Sinking Fund is of all others the most fertile device for aggravating that evil.

MY DEAR DUKE,

HAVING now shortly stated the grounds on which I have presumed to accuse the Committee of gross inconsistency, in recommending to Parliament a line of conduct perfectly unauthorised by the principles they themselves had stated, as fitting to guide and regulate its conduct; it is, in this letter, my intention to submit to you and to the public the reasoning that has irresistibly led me to the conclusion, that the enthusiastic favour with which the establishment of an efficient Sinking Fund has long and almost universally been regarded, uniformly proceeded on a total misconception of the nature of what is called our public debt, and that such an establishment, instead of producing the beneficial results vulgar prejudice has taught the Committee to expect from it, is, in reality, the device of all others that must most effectually aggravate the sole evil the funding system inflicts, which exclusively arises from its producing a rapid alteration in the distribution of the property belonging to the various members of the community.

This opinion, thus broadly and distinctly stated, must at once disclose to you, that I neither mean, with Dr Hamilton, in his Enquiry into the National Debt, to limit my criticism on the past conduct of the Legislature; to the mere assertion of the proposition, that an excess of revenue above expenditure is the only real Sinking Fund by which a public debt can be discharged ; nor, with Lord Grenville, simply to maintain, " that, under no circumstances, any " Sinking Fund can be productive of real benefit, " except where the ordinary income of the state " has been carried to an amount permanently exceed- " ing its current expenditure."

These propositions were, in substance, stated by Mr Fox in the year 1786; and the rectitude of them has been maintained by Dr Hamilton, and, more recently by Lord Grenville, with a degree of anxiety, and at a length, that seems to be unnecessary. To me they long ago appeared self-evident, and, as they are now so considered in the Report of the Committee of the House of Commons, there is no great danger of our in future borrowing to any great extent, for the purpose of sustaining a Sinking Fund, though, after all, when the subject is properly understood, it may perhaps appear the least mischievous mode of effecting it.

Indeed, I am so far from professing myself to be, with Lord Grenville, a disciple of Dr Hamilton's school, or a great admirer of his doctrines, that I never thought he thoroughly understood the subject; and there are certainly very few of the twelve propositions that form the foundation of his reasoning, to which I could accede, though he has assumed them to be so incontrovertible as to make it unnecessary to adduce any argument in their favour.

From the tenets of that school I, in truth, differ to such an extent, as to be disposed to maintain that every interference with the property of the subject, which has for its object to constitute a Sinking Fund, is injurious; and that what they call the only efficient Sinking Fund which can be productive of a real benefit to the state, which involves taxes being either kept up or imposed for the purpose of securing a surplus of revenue over expenditure, is of all others the most injurious; for I think I can, with success, contend that, just in proportion as the amount of revenue so applied is great, the injury to the community must be serious, and that, notwithstanding what has been said by the Committee, it is a matter of perfect indifference, whether the surplus so applied arises from taxes previously existing, or from the produce of taxes imposed for the sole object of producing it.

In thus distinctly stating an opinion I have long

maintained, I must nevertheless freely confess that, if the Committee of the House of Commons had, in their Report, abstained from all argument, and confined themselves, as you have done, to the mere assertion that the salvation of the state depended upon keeping up an efficient Sinking Fund, or, if like Mr Hume in his Essay on Public Credit, they had simply declared the modern practice of mortgaging the public revenue to be ruinous beyond the evidence of a hundred demonstrations, the weight of such authority added to the general prepossessions that I am afraid still exist in the public mind, would have made me despair of success, and induced me to abandon the attempt of convincing either you or the public of the rectitude of those views I am about to submit.

For I am fully aware that all must be desirous of seeing that effected, which such an institution professes to accomplish, and that the belief of its efficacy is founded on doctrines which have been so long, so habitually, and so universally cherished, as even to have regulated and governed the language used in communicating our ideas on the subject from the time our funding system originated. And I am inclined to carry my belief on the subject of the errors and obscurity, the mistakes and confusions that are spread in the world by an ill use of words, further than even Mr Locke; for to me it appears, of all others, the most dangerous source of error, as it is the constant practice of all superficial thinkers, when they find a phrase in general use, at once to regard it as conveying the common testimony of mankind in favour of the reasoning that appears to have suggested it, and thus to adopt from a supposed notion of authority, opinions that a more profound examination of the subject would have made them reject.

With this conviction if the Committee, to whose judgment the public mind had been, for a length of time, trained to look up, as sure to form a sound decision on this question, had relied solely on the authority of their opinion, I feel persuaded that prudence would have taught even the most hardy to trust to time and experience as the only means of correcting the error.

But, fortunately for the cause of truth, they have not dealt in mere assertion, they have not exclusively confided in the weight which their opinion must have had on the minds of men almost universally prejudiced in favour of the common-place view they have taken of the subject. On the contrary, they have boldly ventured to assign reasons for the line of conduct they recommend, and have imprudently attempted by argument to fortify what, if rested on authority, must have been deemed impregnable.

Of the effects of this appeal from authority to reason and argument, it is impossible to entertain a doubt; those, who have hesitated to admit the unqualified praise and the inordinate encomiums which this measure has, for a length of time, commanded, can no longer be borne down by the *dicta* of Dr Price, or Mr Pitt, or by the mere statement that he and Mr Fox, who differed on most questions of general policy, at one time viewed such an establishment with an equal degree of favour.* Even the more powerful fact, that there is no author, nor any public man, from the time of the establishment of Sir Rohert Walpole's Sinking Fund to the present moment (myself excepted), who has not maintained such an application of a real surplus of revenue to be beneficial, can no longer be of avail, far less appear conclusive ; for the moment reason and argument are appealed to, the conclusion must fall to the ground, unless on examination the premises prove unexceptionable, and the reasoning by which it is established is incapable of refutation.

It is fortunate too, that this is, perhaps, the case of all others, in which such an appeal must bring the question in dispute to the most speedy decision ; for there can be no great variety in the argument, arising out of the multiplicity of facts on which it is founded, or from the number and extent of the inferences bearing on the point, which leads to the conclusion that has been so universally acquiesced in ; neither is there to be found in the reasoning of the Committee any novel exercise of ingenuity ; nothing is relied upon that throws any additional light on

* I do not believe that Mr Fox ever publicly retracted the opinions he had given; but, at the time I first published, in 1804, on the subject, I have letters from him, which sufficiently prove that he entertained doubts, and before he died he certainly stated to me his conviction of the rectitude of my opinions.

the subject; for there is not even an attempt to give any new view of the question, that might have a chance of dispelling the scepticism, which is said recently to have shone forth in relation to the advantages of such an establishment.

The frame of the argument relied upon is, that which has exclusively been resorted to by all, who have defended the establishment, from the first institution of a Sinking Fund to effect the redemption of (what is called) our public debt. It consists in advancing propositions, in themselves indisputable truisms, in relation to a debt contracted by a private individual, and then transferring them as alike true and indisputable in the case of what they choose to denominate a public debt, on an unfounded unauthorised assumption, uniformly unsupported by argument, that there is a similarity betwixt the one and the other, which, in reality, in no respect exists.

Proceeding on this principle, the Committee have stated what is perfectly true as applicable to debt, contracted even by the wealthiest individual, that, if his property is subjected to a great permanent annual charge, created by a long continued system of extravagance supported by borrowing, and no effort is made to reduce that charge till the practice of borrowing is again resumed, a perseverance in such improvident conduct must ultimately occasion the fabric of his credit to crumble under the accumulated pressure of his increased and increasing debt.

As applicable to the debt of a private person, this

indeed is a proposition, which (as the Committee say) is too obvious to require an argument. By the expenditure of every sum he borrows, the wealth of an individual is undoubtedly diminished, and, unless his wealth could be supposed to be infinite, it is perfectly clear that, under such management, it must, sooner or later, vanish.

But, if it is true, that the public wealth of a country is the aggregate of the wealth of the individuals of whom the community consists, as long as (what is called) our debt is constituted in the manner heretofore pursued, by borrowing from some members of the community, and raising the interest of the sum so acquired by imposing taxes on other members of the same community, the amount of our national wealth, unlike that of an individual, must obviously remain unimpaired, however frequently this operation may be repeated; for it is nothing to the nation in general, whether the revenue is possessed by one man or by another; to the public, so far as regards their resources, it is a matter of perfect indifference, whether a member of the community possesses the whole revenue arising from his property, or whether his neighbour enjoys an annuity out of it.

If a country owes (to use the vulgar language) two hundred millions, borrowing a hundred millions more will undoubtedly alter the distribution of the property amongst the subjects of the state that has recourse to the operation; it will clearly impoverish and deprive of part of his enjoyments the tax-payer, whilst it will increase to an equal extent the joint receipt of those, who have stipulated for annuities out of the tax imposed in return for their capital advanced, and of those who are paid for their labour in managing the transfer from the tax-payer to the annuitant; but, unless the definition of national wealth hitherto universally received can be proved to be erroneous, as the national wealth includes that of the tax-payers, of the tax-collectors, and of the receiver of the annuity, a transfer of any given sum from the one to the other can never diminish the collective wealth of the whole, in the manner in which the wealth of an individual is diminished by the expenditure of what he acquires by borrowing.

Yet such is the reasoning, if reasoning it can be called, which constitutes not only all this Committee have advanced, but all that has ever been brought forward in the shape of argument to justify the extravagant statement of benefits that have long and universally been considered as the sure result of the steady application of an efficient Sinking Fund. By a strange perversion of everything that seems regular in argument, in announcing the premises, the use of language is assumed, which, if admissible, is decisive of the question in dispute; for you must perceive that to talk of a public debt, is using an expression which cannot be vindicated but on the ground of assuming the justice of that analogy the reasoning pretends to establish betwixt a private debt, and the transaction which gives rise to what is denominated a public debt.

Yet it is the use of this term,—as descriptive of that alteration in the arrangement of property, which arises from imposing a tax upon the means of some of the community, in exchange for the protection afforded to their property by public exertion, as well as that which is occasioned by conveying to others of the community an annuity out of the proceeds of the tax thus imposed in exchange for their having advanced the means of affording that protection, which the expenditure of the sum of money so advanced secures,—that forms the ground-work of all the reasoning which has produced universal misconception on the subject: though a little reflection must have convinced any reasonable man that the transaction, by which a country thus acquires extraordinary means of expenditure, has no resemblance to the contracting of a private debt; in reality, the whole transaction is nothing but conveyances of property from one member of the community to another, which neither gives to the one a right to demand anything more, nor imposes upon the other any future obligation, and which can therefore have no resemblance to a debt contracted by one man's borrowing from another, which at once imposes on the borrower the obligation of restoring what he has received, and gives to the lender the right of demanding repayment.

But, if there is in reality no resemblance which can justify any conclusion from analogy betwixt the obligations that arise out of an individual's contracting debt, and those that are created by the public's acquiring extraordinary means of expenditure, there is certainly still less resemblance, and, of course, a greater impossibility of drawing any such conclusion from the result of the two transactions, as affecting the wealth or riches of those who are parties to them.

A private individual, who borrows capital from another person, acquires the command over it; it becomes appropriated to his own exclusive enjoyment, or to be used for the satisfaction of any desire by which he, the borrower, may be actuated; but the produce of a public loan is appropriated as much for the benefit and security of those who receive the annuity in exchange for the capital advanced, as for that of those who pay the tax out of which the annuity proceeds, and to which the annuitant himself generally contributes.

Whilst, therefore, the annuity thus constituted and the tax imposed, give rise to nothing but a conveyance of property from one description of persons to another,—that is, from those who pay the tax to the annuitant,—which can, in no respect, diminish the total mass of public wealth, the expenditure of the sum advanced, instead of impoverishing the public, as it universally does an individual, who consumes what he borrows, must always add to the wealth of a community, by the encouragement thereby given to additional exertions of industry, the only means of either creating or increasing public wealth.

Thus, it appears, on reflection, impossible for any man to justify that reasoning from analogy, which

identifies the act of an individual contracting debt
with the transfer of property the funding system
occasions. Yet it is on this ground alone the Committee, in their Report, which has been termed one
of the most valuable financial documents ever laid
before Parliament, have described the public as
suffering under the pressure of all those calamities,
to which an individual is exposed who contracts debt,
conceiving that the great alteration in the distribution of property, to which resorting to the funding
system during war gives rise, places a community
in the same situation with an individual who has got
into debt; and they are seemingly so confident in
their opinion of the accuracy of the analogy, as to
have presumed to state that, "if the accumulated
" debt of each period of extraordinary exertion is to
" be handed down undiminished as a load upon
" those, who are thereafter to meet the exigencies
" of other struggles and other difficulties, it is too
" obvious to require an argument that the time can-
" not be very distant, (according to the ordinary
" vicissitudes of peace and war in the history of
" human affairs), when the combined weight of the
" past and present burthens must become too great
" for the most prosperous people to support, and
" the fabric of public credit must crumble under the
" accumulated pressure."

Now it cannot be doubted that this doctrine
conveys to Parliament, and publishes to the world,
under the authority of the respectable names who

compose that Committee, the false, mischievous, and dangerous assertion, that the resources of this country are at this moment impaired. In saying that it is false, mischievous, and dangerous, I certainly do not mean to insinuate that any of the respectable members of that Committee, wilfully asserted what appeared to them either in itself false or dangerous to the interests of their country; but I cannot acquit them of having loosely given credit to common-place inaccurate views of the important subject Parliament had submitted to their consideration, which, if they had been minutely sifted by men even of talents far inferior to theirs, would have forced upon their minds conclusions very different from those contained in the Report.

For it is hardly possible to believe that any man can conceive that the resources of this country are impaired, who does not wilfully shut his eyes to the great increase of production, which was apparent throughout every part of the United Kingdom—to the augmented and annually augmenting accounts of our imports and exports, and to the progressive increase in the consumption of every species of commodity that took place during the supposed diminution of public wealth. And, that such an opinion, falling from such authority, must be dangerous and mischievous, cannot fail to be apparent to all, who, for a moment, reflect on the effect it must have in lowering our importance in the scale of civilized nations. Though, fortunately, it is hardly possible to suppose that any reasoning, or any authority, could convince foreigners that our resources are diminished, at a time when it is universally known that no nation in the world can command extraordinary resources, without applying to this country; and it would be strange indeed, if anything could induce a general belief, that, though we have more ample resources to supply the extraordinary wants of others, than at any former period of our history, there existed some incomprehensible difficulty, if a case of necessity occurred, of exclusively applying those resources to our own use.

That the Committee was placed in a situation of the utmost responsibility cannot be doubted ; the confidence Parliament avowedly reposed in the fruits of their labour, could not fail to excite the utmost exertions on their part; and in the public mind this conviction naturally gave rise to an opinion, that some new information would be brought forward, such as would either reconcile Parliament to abandon a system, that had been so long tried and so often infringed upon, and that has been sometimes praised for its facilitating our contracting debt, sometimes for its power in discharging it ;—or such as would place before them more clear and explicit proof of the benefits to result from persevering in the measure, than had hitherto been derived either from practical experience, or from the theoretical reasoning of those who had made the public finance their peculiar study.

In this, however, the hopes of the country have been completely disappointed, insomuch that, by resting the defence of the measure exclusively on the old ground of the analogy between a private debt, and what is assumed to be a public debt, the Committee have gone far to produce a conviction, that there is no other means of making a plausible argument in favour of this system, which, by promising benefits so much in accordance with the wishes of the country, has so long commanded their approbation.

Indeed I cannot but suspect that this is nearly the truth, and that there is in reality no other means of constructing an argument in support of such an institution; for I am convinced that, though you have as much as most men the praiseworthy habit of thinking for yourself, yet, if you will retrace and examine the process that took place in your own mind, which justified the assertion that the salvation of the state depended upon keeping up an efficient Sinking Fund, you will find it impossible to deny that you was actuated by the idea that there existed so clear an analogy betwixt a private debt and that alteration in the distribution of property, which the world has been taught by habit to call a public debt, as to authorise the conclusion, that all the evils are thereby inflicted on the public, which an individual suffers from contracting debt; and that, of course, to secure the welfare of the state, it became necessary to have recourse to the measure that is certainly the most efficacious in relieving an individual from the ruin a progressive augmentation of his debt must inflict.

Nay more, I will venture to assert, without fear of deliberate contradiction from any well-informed man, that, from the time of Mr Munn's publication, entitled "England's Treasure by Foreign Trade," down to the speech of Mr Canning on opening the budget of the year 1827, there is not to be found an argument in favour of such an establishment, nor an attempt to justify the exaggerated statements of future benefit to be derived from it, that is not founded on the justice of this supposed analogy. The view of the question Mr Munn entertained, which has since universally prevailed, is very clearly expressed in the following passage of his little treatise :—" In the stock of a kingdom, as " in the estate of a private man, who is supposed to " have one thousand pounds yearly revenue, and " two thousand pounds of ready money in his chest ; " if such a man, through excess, shall spend one " thousand five hundred pounds per annum, all his " ready money will be gone in five years ; and in " the like time his said money will be doubled, if he " take a frugal course to spend but five hundred " pounds per annum ; which rule never faileth like-" wise in the commonwealth." And no one, who reads the speech of Mr Canning, can doubt the train of reasoning which passed in his mind, when, after quoting the most wild and unguarded of all Mr Pitt's speeches on the subject, made under the impression that accumulation might be carried to an

indefinite extent, as is evident from the quotation
with which he ended,—" *mobilitate viget, viresque
acquirit eundo,** "—he distinctly declares his opinion,
" that a Sinking Fund of five millions is a proportion
" which never had occurred in his mind, proceeding

---

* I recollect the day after this speech was delivered, the first
Earl of Liverpool, then Lord Hawkesbury, asked me if I had been
in the House of Commons last night; saying that he was told Mr
Pitt had made a most splendid speech. I answered that I had
been there, and that I had retired with astonishment at the igno-
rance Mr Pitt betrayed, in stating Dr Smith to be the first who
had maintained and explained those doctrines on the subject of
capital, and the accumulation thereof, on which he had rested his
argument. Lord Hawkesbury (supposed to be the best-informed
man of his day on these subjects) said, Why, it certainly is so;
where can you find those doctrines detailed before his time?
My answer was, In a hundred publications in this country, a
century before the Wealth of Nations was published, and more
recently in the works of many French authors, particularly in the
treatise of M. Turgot *Sur la Formation et Distribution des Richesses,*
from which Dr Smith was by many supposed to have copied
rather too accurately. When, to my surprise, he told me he never
had heard of the book, which at his desire I sent him next day;
and I now annex a copy of the note with which it was accompa-
nied, when he returned it some time afterwards, the original of
which is bound up with my copy of the treatise :—

" Lord Hawkesbury presents his compliments to Lord Lauder-
" dale, and returns him herewith M. Turgot's tract *Sur la Forma-*
" *tion et Distribution des Richesses,* which he has read with the
" greatest pleasure. It contains all that Mr Adam Smith has
" written on the influence of capital on the commerce of a nation.
" But M. Turgot developes his principles in a more neat and clear
" manner by far than Adam Smith, who appears to have borrowed
" greatly from him.

" *Addiscombe Place, August 24th,* 1793."

" on the analogy of private life, that it would be
" prudent to forego."

Neither is it surprising that this reasoning should
have generally been received with confidence in its
rectitude; for it must be admitted that, however
indefensible and erroneous it must on due consideration appear, it has not only been sanctioned,
but even adopted as sound and incontrovertible
by those who have contended against the establishment of a Sinking Fund formed on the principle on which the Legislature has heretofore proceeded. Thus Dr Hamilton, in his Enquiry into the
rise, progress, and redemption of the national debt,
states " that the progress and discharge of the debt
" of a nation are regulated on the same principles as
" those of an individual;" and, after giving a long
detail of the mode in which an individual should
discharge the debt he has contracted, concludes by
saying, " Substitute millions, or ten millions, for
" thousands, and the reasoning is equally applicable
" to the public debt of a nation." And though Lord
Grenville denies that any direct or immediate gain
belongs to the application of a sum realized by
saving, being used to discharge a public debt, nevertheless he distinctly states, " that a community may
" enrich itself by saving in the same manner as an
" individual," and, of course, he must maintain the
reverse of the proposition, that a community must
impoverish itself by expenditure, and consequent
accumulation of debt.

In this essay, Lord Grenville formally announces

an opinion, that the best of all instruments for the discovery of truth in political economy, is a reference to the transactions in private life, a proposition which can only be true, if the transactions, concerning which we wish to enlighten ourselves or others, are in every respect similar to the circumstances occurring in the case referred to; for it is certainly the most dangerous of all modes of investigation, if there happens to be the least dissimilarity, as in that case there exists neither a more fertile means of self-deception, nor a more plausible mode of enforcing an erroneous conclusion; and perhaps there could not occur a more efficient mode of illustrating this truth than that which the question I am now discussing naturally presents.

For, if the consequences of contracting what is called a public debt are to be decided by reference to the effects that getting into debt produces on the fortune of an individual, most undoubtedly all the calamities the Committee ascribe to a community contracting (what is called) a public debt, must be admitted to be undeniable. But the Committee have forgot that, by the impoverishment of one individual, the opulence of another may be increased, and that the increased wealth of one member of the community generally flows from the diminished wealth of one or more members of the community; nay, that in the case of abstinence from expenditure, and accumulating the sum saved into capital, those, in the produce of whose industry it would otherwise have been expended, must always suffer a diminution of wealth, none of which transactions can, in the least degree, affect public wealth, as the aggregate, of which it is composed, is as much diminished by the loss of the one member of the community, as increased by the gain of the other.

Indeed, so little is there of resemblance betwixt the consequences of an individual's contracting debt, and a nation getting into what it is the habit to call debt, that I mean, in my next Letter, to confine myself to the sole object of endeavouring to satisfy you, that, though an individual always must be impoverished by contracting debt, the extra expenditure that takes place during warfare, and occasions what is called a public debt, has been, and always must be, the most active means of encouraging the increase of production, and of course the most fertile means of promoting the augmentation of the collective wealth of a community.

Should it, however, be thought necessary to found an argument on a reference to private life, it must be admitted that the conclusion is likely to be more accurate, if drawn from circumstances that afford some degree of resemblance to the operation performed by a nation, when it raises funds from one class of its subjects, and discharges the sum acquired, by giving an annuity out of the revenue of another class of its subjects, expending the sum so raised in the purchase of the produce of the country; and in such a case the conclusion will be found very different, for it will illustrate the assertion, that an operation of this nature cannot diminish the gross amount of national wealth, nor impair the resources of a community.

Let us, for example, suppose that in private life six merchants formed a copartnership, each putting a capital of 100,000*l.* into the concern, there can be no doubt that, if one of the partners, from personal extravagance, became obliged to withdraw 10,000*l.* of his capital from the concern, which was immediately supplied by another partner advancing other 10,000*l.* this operation often repeated would greatly alter the distribution of the share of wealth held by the various partners in the firm, but it would never diminish the total wealth of the copartnery, which must consist, as it did at first, of 600,000*l.* and therefore both the resources and the credit of the establishment must remain unimpaired.

In like manner a community, who never borrows but from its own subjects, and always discharges the debt by an annuity raised from its own subjects, expending the sums so levied amongst its own subjects, may, and inevitably will alter the distribution of property existing amongst the various members of the community; but if the national wealth is synonymous with the total wealth of those of whom the community consists, this exchange of equivalents can in no respect diminish the general mass of wealth, and of course cannot impair either the resources or the credit of the country.

In his late Essay on the Sinking Fund, already referred to, Lord Grenville maintains, and unanswerably maintains, that the wealth of a community cannot by the means of such an institution be increased, " because, for every portion of previously-" appropriated wealth, which the Sinking Fund " places at the disposal of the community, it has " withdrawn from the same community a corres-" ponding portion of wealth, previously in the free " disposal of individuals of that community ;" but it is extraordinary he does not seem to have perceived that the very same reasoning proves that, by contracting a debt (as it is called) the public wealth can, in no respect, be impaired ; for, as every portion of revenue, abstracted by taxation, goes either into the pocket of the supposed creditor, or into that of those who are employed in collecting and transferring it to him, and as their wealth forms a portion of the aggregate wealth of individuals, as well as that of the payer of taxes, it follows that the revenue of the former is by borrowing as much increased as the revenue of the latter is diminished, and the aggregate of the wealth of the community, which constitutes public wealth, must remain unimpaired by such a transaction.

With regard to the expenditure of the sum raised by this operation, I think it right for the present to abstain from saying anything. Because, though it is obvious, that passing into the hands of individuals of the community, in exchange for an equivalent value of commodities, or of labour bestowed in services, both necessary for the public defence, public wealth cannot thereby be diminished, the precise effects of this expenditure will come more properly to be investigated subsequently, when I flatter myself I shall succeed in convincing you that, far from diminishing public wealth, it must be, and always has proved, a most fertile means of increasing it.

Such are the considerations that dispose me to give a very different character to the common-place scanty reasoning of the Committee on this branch of the subject, from that with which Lord Bexley has honoured it. For I must think it betrays a careless absence of thought on the important matter referred to them, as it appears to me impossible to read the passage already quoted, without being convinced that it was drawn up under an impression that our resources as well as our credit were impaired, which could not have existed, if the Committee had not been of opinion that the national wealth was diminished ; and that this really was their opinion, is further apparent, from their declaring " that they would have recommended a perse-" verance in the resolution of Parliament in 1819, to " apply five millions annually to the gradual extinc-" tion of our debt, if that measure could have been " accomplished without adding new burdens on the " country."

For they never could have hesitated in recommending the imposition of new taxes to effect a measure calculated, in their opinion, to contribute (as they express it) towards preventing the fabric of our public credit from crumbling under accumulated pressure, if they had taken a just view of the situation of the country, which would have led them to the conclusion,—that though there is perhaps no instance on record of the distribution of property in any community, without civil commotion, undergoing such a formidable change in twenty-four years as took place in this country betwixt the year 1792 and the year 1816, yet the general mass of wealth throughout the community, which is the foundation both of our resources and of our credit, whilst it furnishes the only sure criterion of judging of their extent, never was at any period of our history so great, and of course the fabric of our public credit, if the affairs of the country are judiciously managed, never was in less danger of crumbling under accumulated pressure.

Though I neither entertain the least doubt of the truth of this proposition, nor feel the smallest difficulty in declaring my belief that there is no man, either in or out of the Committee, who will stretch his speculations beyond the sphere of vulgar prejudice, and give himself the trouble of seriously considering the subject, that must not accede to it, when he contemplates the increased fertility of our soil,— the unparalleled augmentation of all our manufacturing establishments,—the extension of our towns from the capital to the meanest village throughout the kingdom,—the wonderful amelioration of all internal communication by canals, railways, and improved roads, as well as the unparalleled increase of our imports and exports which took place during the war.

Yet I must protest against being understood to

have the most remote desire of recommending or encouraging any system of policy, that can have a tendency to place the country in a situation that may lead to renew the scene of extravagant expenditure, which the modern means of conducting warfare renders necessary.

For, though I have been long convinced that it must be a sure receipt for increasing the wealth of a community, for which I will subsequently assign my reasons, there is perhaps no one opinion, from which, during a long political life, I never saw less temptation to deviate, than that which makes me hold that no speculation of future benefit, or of remote security, or indeed anything but the immediate necessity of acting in self-defence, can vindicate the subjecting a community to the danger of dissension and even of revolution, with which a sudden alteration in the distribution of property must always threaten every civilized society.

To the opinions I have long entertained on this subject, you can be no stranger, for I recollect some years ago sending you a copy of a proposed Address to His Majesty, (which I never published) drawn up for the purpose of proving by an appeal to history that there is no record of any popular tumult, insurrection, or revolution in a government, where any degree of liberty had been previously enjoyed, which may not be distinctly traced to an alteration in the distribution of property, nor any transition from tyranny to liberty which does not owe its origin to the same cause.

On that occasion I contended, what I now more than ever firmly believe,—

1st. That all animals are only made to regulate their actions in conformity to the will of another; that is, they are only to be ruled and governed by the management of the objects of their desire.

2d. That men are not exempt from that general law of animal economy, which makes obedience to those who have the controul over the objects of their desire, not a matter of choice but of necessity.

3d. That man cannot obtain dominion over man by the exercise of his reasoning faculties;—because, as it is only in balancing betwixt all his various objects of desire, and in deciding to which he will yield obedience, that reason has any sway in regulating a man's own conduct;—so the efforts of our reasoning powers are subject to a similar limitation when we attempt by reason to regulate the conduct of others.

4th. That the objects of man's desire may be divided into two different classes.—First, That there are objects of desire, which can only be enjoyed by the person to whom they appear desirable, as, for example, life, absence of pain, and sleep; all of which, however desirable to an individual, it is clear cannot be transferred to the use of another; and that the power over this class of the objects of our desire commands obedience solely from the dread of being deprived of them, whilst the deed, which forms the act of obedience, is done in conformity to the will expressed by those who govern, in order to avoid the various interferences with the enjoyments of them, which constitute, punishment.—Secondly, That there are objects of desire, which may be enjoyed alike by every human being, the enjoyment of which may be transferred to, or shared with our fellow creatures: That this last class forms the description, and the real definition of what, in civilized society, is called property: and that, from the command over this class of the objects of man's desire, obedience is far more frequently volunteered in consequence of the hope of participating in those objects of desire which are possessed by others, than it is secured by the dread of being deprived of what a man himself possesses; whilst in either case, the deed, which forms the act of obedience, proceeds directly from the will of the person governed, in the hope of securing to himself a reward.

5th. That the management of these two classes of the objects of man's desire are the only two sources of power commanding obedience, and that, when these two sources of power are so arranged that the power emanating from both duly co-operate, peace and contentment uniformly prevail in every community; and that, when, on the contrary, these two sources of power are in a state of discordancy, irritation and dissatisfaction are always manifested, which generally terminate in a display of turbulence and in attempts to effect a revolution.

With a thorough belief in the rectitude of these general principles, I have long looked at the history of our times, without any difficulty in discerning the causes of that change in the general feelings of the people of this country with regard to their political institutions, which, however calamitous, appeared only the natural consequence of what has taken place.

The vast alteration in the distribution of property, which the unparalleled extent of the transfer of wealth during the last war from the tax-payer to the stock-holder occasioned, has, in a great measure, put an end to that fortunate state of things, in which the power emanating from property acted naturally and forcibly in aid of the constituted power of the state, by uniting the inducement to obedience afforded by the prospect of securing a benefit, the means by which power emanating from property always acts, to the mandate of Government enforced by penalties. A state of things that created an inclination to obey, and gave therefore to Government, at the moment it acted with the greatest energy, a character of want of severity and of mildness, which, more than anything else, attaches the subjects of a state to its political institutions.

With these strong impressions of the deep injury the country has sustained from the unparalleled change that has taken place in the distribution of property;—a subject which would lead me into great details, were I to go into the consideration of the effects it has had, in my own time, on the constitution of both Houses of Parliament : as well as on the direction given to the industry of the community;—I can assure you, that, however strong my conviction may be (for which I will subsequently assign my reasons at large), that a real Sinking Fund must always diminish the wealth of a community, I should be an eager supporter of such an establishment, if I could really believe that a Sinking Fund tends, as some have maintained, to restore the sums withdrawn from the property of the members of the community to those to whom it antecedently belonged.

Because, in that case, I should regard it as the means of restoring that connection betwixt the constituted authority and the power emanating from property, which so long dictated to the people of this country that admiration so generally expressed of its political institutions, and therefore as affording a sure remedy for what I consider to be the main, nay, I may say, the only evil, which what the Committee denominates contracting debt inflicts on a community.

But to me this view of the subject appears so thoroughly false and unfounded, that I must, on the contrary, regard a Sinking Fund as a means of producing further and far more rapid alterations in the distribution of property. For I do not hesitate to assert, that the alterations which must take place if a Sinking Fund, such as the Committee applaud, is persevered in, will be in themselves more formidable and ruinous than what would have ensued from continuing the practice of (what is called) contracting debt.

I doubt not that this opinion will at first view appear to you questionable. I know it is in direct opposition to the doctrines commonly maintained on the subject, and that it must be regarded as unintelligible by all who, seemingly without examination, certainly without any reason assigned, have carelessly adopted the vulgar prejudices, which so pre-eminently shine forth in the Report of the Committee. Nevertheless it is unquestionably true; and in confidently pronouncing on its justice and accuracy, I do not solely rely upon general theoretical reasoning; for I feel that an appeal may be made, with perfect security, to the inferences which experience of the consequences that have ensued in all cases, where the establishment of a Sinking Fund has been resorted to, must force on every reflecting mind. Nay, I am confident that, if the Committee themselves will calmly consider the facts they have stated, and the admissions they have made in their Report, they cannot resist acceding to the truth of the assertion.

Now, in pursuing this branch of the subject, I will, for the present, set aside all consideration of the question, whether a Sinking Fund tends, as some think, to enrich a country, or, as I shall subsequently maintain, to impoverish it, or whether, as some have contended, it effects a mere exchange of equivalents, which can neither enrich nor impoverish any community; and I will endeavour shortly to trace and explain to you the effects a real efficient Sinking Fund, established for counteracting the bad effects of (what is called) our debt, must have in altering the distribution of property in every country that resorts to such an establishment.

For this purpose let us suppose that there had in any country, in consequence of great extra expenditure during war, been created (what is called) a large public debt, which in three per cents amounted to a sum of five hundred millions, in four per cents to the sum of eighty millions, and a further debt in five per cents to the amount of one hundred and fifty millions.

Let us further suppose, that the Government of the country so situated, proceeding upon what Mr Canning termed the analogies of private life, thought it necessary to have a real efficient Sinking Fund of five millions. And that, for this purpose, they enacted, or retained laws unrepealed, enacting taxes to the annual amount of five millions, beyond the ordinary expences of the state, including the interest of what is called its debt, further providing that this sum should be annually paid into the hands of Commissioners, to be by them expended as capital in the purchase of the greatest revenue they could obtain in the public annuities.

Under this hypothesis it must be at once apparent, and that beyond the possibility of dispute, that the first and obvious consequence of such an arrangement would be the conversion of five millions raised by taxation from the revenue of the community, into capital, which would add to that extent to the existing sum of capital in the country ; for, though the offers of advanced price by the Commissioners, into whose hands these five millions would be transferred, must tempt the stock-holders to sell that portion of

stock the Commissioners are by law under the necessity of acquiring, it could afford no inducement to
the stock-holders to expend as revenue the capital
they had received in exchange for the stock transferred, or, in other words, to ruin themselves to
counteract the effects that might result from such a
sudden forced increase of capital.

The stock-holder would therefore naturally look
out for some other channel, in which he could vest
his capital, so as to secure an annual revenue, and
this could only be done, if he himself intended
to use the capital, by lowering the rate of profit
attending the duties he devoted it to perform, and
thus forcing out of employment a share of the capital
previously engaged in executing these duties;—or,
if the person who has sold the stock and acquired
the capital, means to lend it out to be used by others,
he must force it into employment by lowering the
interest he is contented to receive, so as to enable
those who use it to diminish the profits on the duties
they employ it in performing.

Now, without attempting to define the specific
effect this operation, annually repeated, must have in
any given space of time, it cannot be doubted that
ere long the market rate of interest must, from the
increased and increasing abundance of capital, be
reduced from five to three per cent., and of course
the Government of the community, as in duty
bound, must reduce the interest paid on four per
cents and five per cents to three per cent., which,
in the supposed case, will take out of the pockets of

that class of the community, who hold the sum of eighty millions of four per cents, an annual income of eight hundred thousand pounds, being one per cent. on their capital, and out of the pockets of those who are supposed to hold the one hundred and fifty millions of five per cents, an annual income of three millions, being two per cent. on their capital, making together a diminution in the incomes of those who hold property in the supposed four and five per cent. funds of three millions eight hundred thousand pounds, which, taking the interest of capital to be three per cent. is equivalent to a capital of one hundred and twenty-six millions, six hundred and sixty-six thousand, six hundred and sixty-six pounds.

On the other hand, as on the supposition of the market rate of interest having fallen from five to three per cents, the value of three per cent. stock must have risen from sixty to one hundred, this operation must have put into the pockets of those who hold the supposed sum of five hundred millions of three per cents, the sum of two hundred millions, being the difference of value of five hundred millions three per cents taken at sixty, on the supposition of the market rate of interest being at five per cent., and its value on the supposition of the market rate of interest falling to three per cent., in which case it would be at par.

Thus it must evidently appear that this institution, established for the purpose of counteracting the bad effects of that alteration in the distribution of property, which I will subsequently prove to you, is the only bad effect of (what we call) contracting a public debt, must, on all general principles, co-operate with it in increasing the mischief, by making still more formidable alterations in the existing distribution of wealth in this supposed community.

Neither are these the only grounds on which an alteration in the distribution of property must, under such circumstances, take place; for it is obvious that a reduction in the interest of capital, arising from the abundance of it, which by law is thus forcibly created, would of necessity take also from the income of all those who had capital lent out on personal or landed security, two-fifths of their revenue; whilst, on the other hand, it would give to all those who owed money two-fifths of what they annually paid for the interest of the capital they had borrowed. Besides, the general reduction of interest, making disposable capital less valuable, would inevitably add to the value of land, and every other fixed security, thus enriching all those who had fixed incomes, from whatever source derived, on the same principle that the value of capital vested in three per cents was raised.

It is certain, too, that the abundance of capital, and the reduced profit to be derived from it, must, from the desire generally prevalent amongst capitalists of preventing the diminution of their incomes, give rise to schemes and projects for acquiring greater profits than, under these circumstances, they could, in the ordinary course of transactions, obtain, and that the redundancy of credit, which must always attend this state of things, could not fail to co-operate in involving the country in a scene of speculation that uniformly terminates in the sudden acquisition of wealth by a designing few, and in great losses sustained by the simple and undesigning, who, guided by their hopes and their wishes, are sure to embark in such undertakings.

In short, it seems evident, that such a system could not be long persevered in, without giving to the attentive observer distinct proofs that a Sinking Fund is a more active means of altering the distribution of property, than what is called contracting debt; to remedy the bad effects of which in altering the distribution of property, which will be proved to be its only bad effect, is the reason given for resorting to it.

It is not pretended that this hypothetical case, assumed for the purpose of explaining the mode in which an efficient Sinking Fund must operate in altering the distribution of property, can lead to any accurate or definite conclusion in relation to the precise extent to which, under the circumstances stated, such an establishment would alter it, in any community where it was resorted to.

At the same time, the consequences here attributed to such a legislative arrangement are no ways imaginary, for there is no record of any Sinking Fund, even of far less efficiency than what is here hypothetically assumed to exist, which has not, in a very short time, reduced the interest of capital, by adding to its abundance, and which must not therefore have produced, in a greater or smaller degree, the changes which, in this hypothetical case, are described as likely to take place.

Thus, when Pope Innocent XI reduced the interest of his debt from four to three per cent. and employed the sum saved to accumulate, but a short time elapsed till the new three per cent. fund sold at one hundred and twelve.

Again, when the interest of what was called the National Debt of England was reduced in 1717, from six to five per cent. and the saving devoted to accumulation, the consequence was, that in 1727, from the rise of public securities, there was an opportunity of again reducing the interest from four to three per cent., and of applying an additional sum to accumulate. This, of course, produced another rise; and to such a degree, that in the year 1733, we learn from authority, " That the Sinking Fund was now " grown to a great maturity, and produced annually " about 1,200,000*l*, and was become almost a terror " to all the individual proprietors of the public debt. " The high state of credit, the low rate of interest of " money, and the advanced price of all public stocks " and funds above par, made the great monied com- " panies and all their proprietors apprehend nothing " more than being obliged to receive their principal " too fast; and it became almost the universal con-

" sent of mankind that a million a-year was as much
" as the creditors of the public would bear to receive
" in discharge of part of their principal."*

Further, it is within the recollection of many now
alive that, from the year 1787 to the year 1792,
during which time Mr Pitt contended that he had an
efficient Sinking Fund of one million a-year, three
per cents gradually rose from about seventy-four to
ninety ; a fact which sufficiently illustrates the same
principle; though undoubtedly, there being at that
time a much smaller debt, and much less wealth
throughout the community to operate upon than
what has since existed, the effects of such an establishment could not be so apparent.

For so unfounded are the conclusions drawn by
Messrs Canning and Huskisson from the analogies
of private life, which made the one assert that a
Sinking Fund ought to be great in proportion to the
expenditure,† and the other in proportion to the debt
of a country, ‡ that if alteration in the distribution of
property is a serious evil, a Sinking Fund to the
same extent will produce a much more extensive
alteration in the distribution of property, in a
country where (what is called) the debt is large, and
the wealth and consequent expenditure great, than

---

* Considerations concerning the Public Funds, the Public
Revenues, and the Annual Supplies, by Sir Robert Walpole, p. 56.
 † See Mr Canning's Speech, already quoted.
 ‡ See Mr Huskisson's Speech, July 15, 1828.

it can do in a country where both the wealth and debt are comparatively small.

For the powers of a Sinking Fund in altering the distribution of property depend neither on the extent of the revenue nor on the extent of the debt; they must always be great in proportion to the amount of the Sinking Fund; and in proportion to the amount of wealth enjoyed by the community, in which it is established, as a Sinking Fund to the same amount must produce a much greater alteration in the state of property in a wealthy than in a poor country; and suppose two communities to enjoy a similar degree of wealth, then a Sinking Fund will alter the distribution of property in each, just in proportion to its magnitude.

The last of these propositions seems to be so obvious as to require no illustration, and it appears impossible that a very short explanation should not make the accuracy of the first equally apparent.

Let us suppose two communities, the one poor, with a small amount of public securities, the other comparatively rich, with a large amount of public securities. If in both, the market rate of interest, that is, the price of capital, was the same, (suppose five per cent,) that would certainly satisfactorily show that in both these communities the proportion betwixt the existing demand for capital and the existing supply of it must be nearly the same; for the price of every commodity in every community depends on the proportion betwixt the supply and the demand for it; that is, on the proportion betwixt that part of the commodity that is brought to the market, which forms the effectual supply, and that quantity of it for which there exists a desire on the part of those who have the means of gratifying it, which Dr Smith has properly defined to be the effectual demand.

Under such circumstances, an additional capital of a million thrown into the market, to find employment by means of a Sinking Fund, would in each produce an overflow to that extent; for it is with capital, and with all other commodities, as it is with liquids: if a vessel is full, it matters not whether it contains a gallon or a hundred gallons, a pint added in either case would equally occasion the overflow of a pint: so, if the supply of capital is adjusted in any two countries to the demand for it in similar proportions,—which accordance in the market rate of interest, that is, in its price, always denotes,—the alteration in the price of capital would be similar; but the effect of such an alteration would be much more formidable in producing an alteration in the distribution of property in a rich than in a poor country.

To illustrate this, let us suppose that there existed in any community a debt in three per cents to the amount of two hundred millions, a debt in four per cents to the amount of twenty millions, a debt in five per cents to the amount of fifty millions, and that the capital invested in land was conceived to be of value one hundred millions, and the remaining capital in manufactures and other employment sixty millions.

Again, in another community, let us suppose that there existed a debt in three per cents, amounting to four hundred millions, a debt in four per cents to the amount of forty millions, a debt in five per cents to the amount of one hundred millions; that the capital invested in land was to be conceived to be of value two hundred millions, and the remaining capital in manufactures and other employments one hundred and twenty millions.

Let us further suppose that, in each of these two countries, a million a year was invested in the hands of Commissioners as an accumulating fund for the purpose of discharging what is vulgarly called debt, but what is in reality annuities, sold by each individual, who contributes to the purchase of them, in shares proportioned to his contribution, which annuities are paid out of taxes raised from the community in exchange for the protection afforded to them or to their property.

If the interest of money was the same in both of these two countries, (say five per cent.) then, the proportion betwixt the actual supply and the effectual demand being the same, in each the million must have the same effect at first, in lowering the interest; but, in the progress of accumulation, it would produce a much stronger effect, and consequently the alteration in the distribution of property would be much greater in the more wealthy community.

It is needless to go through details of the difference that would take place, but let us suppose that in each (which, by the bye, would happen at very different periods) the interest of money had fallen from five to three per cent, the effect of this (as it is always considered to be the duty of Government to reduce the annuity, payable out of the taxes, as low as possible) would be,—in the first of these countries to deprive the holders of four and five per cents of a revenue of one million two hundred thousand pounds per annum ; that is, of two hundred thousand pounds, being one per cent on the twenty millions of four per cents reduced to three per cent, and one million on the fifty millions of five per cents, the interest of which would also be reduced to three per cent.

On the other hand, to the property of those of the community, who, by the hypothesis, held two hundred millions of three per cents, as the diminution of the interest of money from five to three would immediately bring their property to par, there would be an addition of eighty millions, being the difference of value betwixt two hundred millions of three per cents at sixty and two hundred millions of three per cents at par. It is obvious too that, on the same principle, this reduction of interest would, in a similar degree, augment the value of the capital of all those of the community possessing fixed income, either from land or any other source, to a sum equal to two-thirds of the capital they were assumed to have so vested.

But, under the state of property which has been supposed to exist in the second commu-

E

nity, the alteration in the distribution of property would be infinitely greater; because, proceeding on the same principle, the loss to the holders of five and four per cents would be two millions four hundred thousand pounds per annum; that is, four hundred thousand pounds on the forty millions of four per cents reduced to three, and two millions pounds on the one hundred millions of five per cents also reduced to three per cents.

On the other hand, there would, in this case, be an addition to the value of the capital of those, who held the four hundred millions of three per cents of one hundred and sixty millions, being the difference of value betwixt four hundred millions of three per cents at sixty, and four hundred millions of three per cents at par; and on the same principle, and in the same proportion, it would add to the property of all those, who, under such circumstances, possessed fixed incomes, either from land, or any other source; and thus, under these two hypothetical cases, both the losses sustained and the gains acquired would be twice as great in the latter as in the former case.

These hypothetical cases are stated for the purpose of at once shewing the folly of thinking that the extent of a Sinking Fund can with prudence or with safety be proportioned either to the expenditure or to the debt of a country: and of conveying a clear view of the important principle, on which it is asserted that the same amount of Sinking Fund will produce a much more formidable alteration in the distribution of property in a very wealthy than in a comparatively poor country; and it would have been needless to have resorted to any assumed or hypothetical case for that purpose, if, amongst the numerous inconsistent financial operations that have taken place since the peace, and the innumerable views of them, detailed in accounts framed to support the favourite plan of the day, it had been possible to make out a plain distinct statement of what was in each year the amount of the surplus of revenue, over the amount of the expenditure defrayed and of the debt directly or indirectly contracted, which was devoted to what has been called redemption of debt,—for that alone, it is now admitted even by the advocates of the system, can constitute what they denominate a real efficient Sinking Fund.

But it is not an easy operation, without official aid, to trace throughout such a number of years the real efficient Sinking Fund, if any existed, that was annually applied to what is called the redemption of debt. For it would be necessary in each year separately to develope and explain the effects,—of the appropriation of balances in the Exchequer, gradually brought to account,—of sums applied to public works, part of which is repaid, part outstanding, and of which another part never will be repaid,—of sometimes increasing the unfunded debt for the purpose of diminishing the funded, and at others increasing the funded debt to diminish the unfunded,—as well as those of occasionally granting annuities in exchange for stock received,—and of loading posterity with the payment of what we ought to discharge, whilst we are burdening ourselves to relieve them from charges, which, in the natural order of things, ought to fall upon them.

Neither would all these facts, if distinctly made out, be sufficient to authorise an accurate conclusion, as it would require an investigation into the sums lost, by adventurers in the schemes to which this abundance of capital gave rise, as well as into the sums lost by those who, from the same cause, sent their capital abroad in quest of larger interest, in the shape of foreign loans, on which the payment even of interest has been suspended; in order to ascertain to what extent the natural operation of the forced increase of our capital was by these means counteracted.

I am certain therefore you will not be surprised that I should hesitate in undertaking such a task, more particularly when you recollect that, with the full power of commanding every official aid, the Committee have declined making the attempt, stating " that it would be extremely difficult to exhibit to " the House a very clear account of the various opera- " tions, including the purchases by this Sinking " Fund, through which the whole reduction made in " the public debt since the peace has been effec- " ted."—But in truth it is not necessary; for whilst the cases I have hypothetically assumed to exist, with the reasoning founded on them, must sufficiently explain the view I entertain of the effects of a real efficient Sinking Fund, in altering the distribution of property, without entering into minute details, the summary view the Committee has enabled us to take of what has happened since the beginning of the year 1816, must place the rectitude of my speculations on that subject beyond all reasonable ground of doubt.

By the Committee the surplus of income above our expenditure, applicable to the diminution of debt has been stated to be 20,753,545*l.* which (as they say) has been swelled by the application of 11,236,824*l.* part of a large balance in the Exchequer, making the sum actually applied for that purpose in twelve years ending the 5th January 1828, 31,990,369*l.*; of the exact amount of this sum applied in each year they have declined giving any account, but we know that at times there was no real surplus, and at others none except what was derived by an application of a part of the balance in the Exchequer, at the commencement of that period; yet nevertheless we have the authority of the Committee for saying that, by the year 1824, the interest of five and of four per cents and of exchequer bills had been, by that means, reduced to an extent that diminished the income of the holders of those securities 2,092,078*l.*; in short, that class of stockholders have been deprived of income to an amount that would have sold at the present price of three per cents for nearly seventy millions of that stock. *

In attributing this reduction of interest solely to

---

* This is taking the 3 per cents at 87.

the establishment of a Sinking Fund, I am not singular, for however much in other respects, I may disagree with the opinions contained in the reports of this Committee, I certainly have the pleasure of enjoying the sanction of those who composed it, in ascribing this alteration in the distribution of property to the Sinking Fund; for you, I am sure, will agree with me in thinking that I do not misrepresent what they have stated when I remind you that they have formally announced, " that although the application " of the surplus revenue above mentioned has affected " only the smallest part of this diminution, yet it " would be difficult to say that, without the con- " tinued application of a portion of the revenue to " the redemption of the existing debt, that increased " value in the public securities would have been " created ; whereby this great alleviation of the " public burthens has been effected."

But whilst the alterations in the market rate of interest produced, as is stated by the Committee, from forced accumulation of a portion of our revenue into capital, seems clearly to have deprived those who held property in five per cents, in four per cents, and in Exchequer bills of this immense proportion of their wealth, it certainly added a much more formidable sum, to the property of those who held the five hundred and thirty millions of three per cents, which was nearly the amount of that stock in the year 1824 : for on an average of the quarter ending the 5th of July of that year, we find three per cent. stock had risen to 95 from 61, the price it bore on an average of the quarter ending the 5th of April 1816, which secured to the proprietors of that stock an advance on their property of no less than 180,200,000*l.*, for that is the difference in value betwixt five hundred and thirty millions of three per cents at 61, and five hundred and thirty millions of the same stock at 95.* And that this state of the money market must have had a similar effect in adding to the capital of all those of the community who possessed fixed income from other sources, I have the authority of the Chancellor of the Exchequer for asserting, when he, on the 1st of June 1821, stated "that the great increase that had taken place " in the value of funded property must increase the " value of all other descriptions of property in the " country, as must be felt in the cases of mortgage " as well as of sales of land :" indeed he might have

---

* The gain on three per cents is here calculated, by taking the difference betwixt the average price of that stock in the quarter immediately after the peace, and the average of the quarter in the year 1824, when the price was at the highest. If similar calculations were made throughout the whole period that has elapsed since the peace, shewing the effect of the alterations in price, arising from the forced accumulation of revenue into capital, and from the diminution created by the devices to acquire larger interest in schemes, projects, and foreign loans, to which such accumulation naturally gave rise, it would exhibit a scene of fluctuation in the value of capital ruinous to all, except to the jobbers and speculators, whose interest it never could have been intended to promote, as their profits are always derived from the losses of the honest and industrious. Yet this is obviously the natural consequence of the system that has been pursued.

added, to the value of all property so vested as to produce a fixed income.

With such a superabundance of capital, however, as this advanced price of all fixed securities must have created, and such a diminution of the market rate of interest, as is the inevitable consequence of a great excess in the supply of capital, in proportion to the demand for it, it is impossible not at once to discern that there must have existed a great facility of commanding credit, and that this, combined with the desire of increasing income, generally so much reduced, in proportion to the capital it could command, must inevitably have given rise to all sorts of projects and schemes of adventure, to increase the revenue on this superabundant capital. Indeed there is no one capable of reflection, possessing the experience of what took place, under similar circumstances, in the cases of the Mississippi and South Sea Schemes, who must not have anticipated, as the result of this state of our affairs, such an extent of bankruptcy and calamity as, whilst it exhausted the supply of capital, and of course increased the demand for it, was sure to produce a sudden and formidable augmentation in the market rate of interest, and, for a time, to extinguish that feeling of prosperity which the anticipation of great imaginary future profits, and the increased demand for commodities—necessary to set those wild projects of gain a-going, as well as to furnish the means of remitting foreign loans—must have excited.

Now it really appears impossible either for you,

or any unprejudiced man, to look back at the facts the economical history of this country displays, immediately after this unparalleled increase of capital and diminution of interest, which the Committee admit was occasioned by the operation of the Sinking Fund, without perceiving that it is in truth an accurate record of those things having happened; which the theory here relied upon must have led us to expect; for it is impracticable to deny that, in the beginning of the year 1824, (when the reduction of interest and augmentation of capital took place, which notoriously gave rise to schemes and speculations, as well as to the unfortunate speculations in American loans, that for a time created an extra demand for the produce and labour of the community,) there existed that general feeling of prosperity which was so emphatically described in his Majesty's Speech from the throne, where it is stated, " That our agricul- " ture, our commerce, and our manufactures, were " in a flourishing state; and that at no former period " of our history did there ever prevail throughout all " the classes of the community in this island a more " cheerful spirit of order, or a more just sense of the " advantages, which, under the blessing of Provi- " dence, they enjoyed."

Neither does it terminate here; for we must perceive that the events, which this excess of adventure arising from the artificial state of property was sure to produce, were accurately realized in the scenes of bankruptcy and distress arising from the failure of the schemes and projects, by which this state of the times enabled designing adventurers thoroughly to ruin many, whose sufferings by the diminution of interest led them thoughtlessly into the snare, from a natural desire of having the means of commanding those enjoyments, to which they had been previously habituated.

We have seen too that this state of calamity, with the severe losses it produced, completely counteracted that growing superabundance of capital, and that a consequent elevation in the interest of money naturally flowed from the temporary derangement, and that to an extent that the loss to the proprietors of three per cent. stock, by the fall that took place in the year 1825, seems to have amounted to nearly fifty-three millions.

After this unfortunate revulsion in the state of our pecuniary concerns took place, we must also recollect that, in consequence of the remedies administered to allay the general feeling of distress, of which the origin seemed unknown,—such as the repeal of taxes,—the strange attempt to throw part of our burdens on posterity,—and other contradictory palliatives, —the Sinking Fund gradually vanished, so that in the year 1827, there existed no real cash surplus; for in that year we are informed the revenue was insufficient by the sum of 127,000*l.* to defray the 612,000*l.* life annuities, with which the Sinking Fund was burdened. In short, since the crisis occurred in the year 1825, in consequence of the failure of those schemes and projects, and losses by foreign loans, in which the people of this country were induced to embark, by the reduction of interest the Sinking Fund had occasioned, there have existed such con-

stant fluctuations in our manufacturing, mercantile, and monied concerns, as induced the most
intelligent member of the Finance Committee to
announce the impossibility of forming any accurate
idea of the probable future receipt of revenue,
from the average of the three last years; whilst
there has prevailed such an universal feeling of
distrust and want of confidence, as has created in the
minds of those in possession of capital, a previously
unknown disinclination permanently to embark it in
any particular employment, so that there existed for
a time an unparalleled amount of capital allowed
to lie dormant in the Bank.

But, if the expenditure of thirty-one millions of
our revenue in the shape of a Sinking Fund has occasioned such an alteration in the interest of money,
as, on the authority of the Committee, is here stated,
and, if the crisis by this means produced in the year
1825, effected that convulsion and subsequent
fluctuation in the mercantile and manufacturing concerns of the country—which Mr Herries says, is
alone sufficient to baffle any computations concerning
the receipt of our revenue on an average of the three
last years—a Sinking Fund must certainly appear a
very mistaken means for remedying that alteration
in the distribution of property which warfare occasions : for I think I have made it perfectly obvious
that a Sinking Fund always must produce a great
alteration in the distribution of property in every
country where it is established, and that, consistent with the admissions of the Committee, it is

impossible to deny that a greater alteration in the distribution of property has been effected in twelve years, ending the 5th of January 1828, by the expenditure of this thirty-one millions of Sinking Fund than would have been produced by five times the amount raised by loan and expended in the conduct of warfare.*

---

* I am aware that much of the suffering here stated has been attributed to the alteration in the value of our currency, to which, in the course of these Letters, I have made no allusion : not because I am not sensible of the mischievous effects that the depreciation of our currency produced : for I cannot forget that in the year 1813, when the Bank note was of value 14s. 8d., I published a proposal to lower the standard by coining fifteen shillings' worth of silver into twenty shillings, and at once resuming cash payments, making that coin a legal tender ; which would have had the immediate effect of giving to every man in possession of, or who had a right to receive, a Bank note a bonus of four pence, and the ultimate effect of relieving the country of one-fourth of its debt. Neither have I forgotten that, since that period, many of those who, at that time, censured this measure, have since proposed, as a remedy for the sufferings of the country, (of the causes of which they were profoundly ignorant,) to reduce the standard, and that at a time when paper had recovered its value, so as to be at par with coin—a measure very different from giving a bonus to the holder of notes in 1813, as it would have been in that case an act of direct confiscation. In truth, however, the calamitous state of things, which has been here alluded to, cannot be regarded as in any respect connected with the state of our currency. At the time the Bill passed in 1819, which is often falsely accused of having produced injurious effects by adopting a system of gradually introducing payments in cash, there existed only four per cent. difference betwixt paper and gold; and it ought to be recollected that the extreme depreciation of paper only took

It is on these grounds I venture to assert that, far from forming a means for redressing the evil, which a war expenditure inflicts, by altering the distribution of property, a Sinking Fund is the most powerful engine that can be devised for aggravating the calamity; and yet I feel confident that, in my next letter, I will satisfy you, and every man whose prejudices will permit him to listen to reason, that this is the only evil which arises out of a war expenditure, and that in truth the financial operation of contracting, (what is called) a public debt, in effect only conveys from the pockets of one part of the community wealth, which it places in the pockets of another part of the same community; whilst, by the great extra expenditure it empowers the Government to sustain, it creates a demand for labour and produce, and a consequent encouragement to exertions of industry, which cannot fail to enrich any community in which it takes place.

I know very well that the constant resort, that has so long and so universally been had to the analogies of private life, in reasoning on this subject, has led

---

place in the three or four last years of the war, and that, in truth, those who suffered loss from the great elevation of our standard before the year 1819, and the trifling elevation that has since taken place, received indemnity by the repeal of taxes in the year 1816 to the extent of 18,700,000*l.*; and, though afterwards 3,000,000*l.* of taxes were imposed, other reductions of taxations have been made, leaving a balance of taxes repealed since the war, to the extent of 17,000,000*l.*

all public men, as well as all who have published upon it, to conceive that our expenditure in warfare is ruinous to our resources—which they maintain (resting on the same analogies) can alone be recruited by diminution of expenditure and future saving. But after many years' deliberation, I have formed a most decided opinion that there is so little ground for relying on any conclusions derived from the analogies of private life as bearing on this subject, that I feel confident I can state to you reasons unanswerable for thinking, that whilst parsimony or abstinence from expenditure for the purposes of accumulating revenue into capital, is the surest receipt for augmenting the wealth of an individual, it is the most active of all means, of diminishing the collective wealth of a community, and that whilst extravagance and extra expenditure, is the surest mode of ruining an individual, great extra expenditure is the most certain means of enriching a community.

Yours, &c. &c. &c.

LAUDERDALE.

LETTER III.

*Details the reasoning, which leads to the conclusions—
that great extra expenditure, provided for by funding,
always has increased, and always must increase the
collective wealth of a community,—and that a Sinking
Fund, which proceeds upon the principle of forcibly
abstracting a portion of the revenue from expenditure
and converting it into capital, always has diminished,
and always must diminish it.*

My dear Duke,

In my last letter I have anxiously endeavoured
to impress on your mind the extreme inaccuracy of
the reasoning universally resorted to, which rests
the expediency of establishing an efficient Sinking
Fund on the analogies of private life; arguing on
that ground that such an establishment forms the
only remedy for the alteration in the distribution of
property, which, providing for the expences of warfare by the modern system of funding, effects, and
maintaining that it operates as a means of restoring
to its original proprietors that revenue, which was
withdrawn from them by subjecting them to taxation in time of war.

Indeed I have gone further, for I have attempted to convince you and the public, that, far from being an instrument useful for effecting the desired end, a Sinking Fund is, on the contrary, the most active of all devices that could be resorted to, for aggravating the evil it is intended to redress, being in truth a means of altering the distribution of the property of a community in the time of profound peace more efficacious than the funding system is in time of war.*

To assume that I have argued this proposition in a manner, which is sure of carrying conviction to your mind, or to that of any man, who was not a member of the Committee of Finance, would be unpardonable arrogance and presumption; but I

---

* Mr Hume, in his Essay on Public Credit, states that it has been contended the public is no weaker upon account of its debts; since they are due amongst ourselves, and bring as much property to one as they take from another. That it is therefore like transferring money from the right hand to the left; against the truth of this view of the subject he argues at some length, and sums up by saying that there is something, therefore, in the case beside the mere transferring of property from one hand to another, and what that is, he very abruptly explains by saying, "In 500 years, the " posterity of those now in the coaches and of those upon the boxes " will probably have changed places, without affecting the public " by these revolutions."

Now this is, in truth, avowing an opinion accurately the same with that which has been here maintained, that the only injurious effect of what is called a public debt, is altering the distribution of property amongst the members of the community.

must be allowed to say, that it appears to me very difficult to discover, how those who concurred in framing and adopting the Fourth Report of that Committee, can with consistency or justice, deny the accuracy of the conclusions I have drawn : for after ascribing to the Sinking Fund the merit of reducing the interest paid out of the revenue raised by taxation on the four per cents, on the five per cents, and on exchequer bills, they can neither with consistency deny its influence in reducing the interest of all other capital lent out on private security which experienced a similar diminution, nor its efficacy in augmenting the value of all capital vested either in three per cents, in land, or in any other security, in which it permanently commands a fixed income; for that follows as an undeniable consequence of that power of reducing interest, which they have admitted it to possess.

Till, therefore, they can point out a means of employing 31,990,369*l.* of capital, in such a manner as to deprive, within a similar compass of time, one part of the community of property to the amount of more than double what has been devoted to this efficient Sinking Fund, and that has at the same time had the effect of giving to another portion of the community, property far exceeding six times the amount of what the Committee has informed us was the real surplus appropriated to the maintenance of a Sinking Fund, I must flatter myself that my reasoning cannot have failed in making an impression on the intelligent minds of the authors of that Report, which has been denominated the most valuable financial document ever submitted to Parliament.

I am however fully aware, that by far the most arduous part of the task I have prescribed to myself remains to be fulfilled; for, in this Letter, I have undertaken to repel a more dangerous inference from the analogies of private life, which seems alike to have tainted the opinions of all who, either in or out of Parliament, have discussed the subject of a Sinking Fund, whether they professed themselves admirers of Mr Pitt's plan, or adherents of Dr Hamilton and Lord Grenville, who have successfully reprobated the details of it.—By all, the arrangements made for defraying the expenses of modern war have been regarded as impoverishing a community; the means raised by imposing taxes on some, and pledging the produce of those taxes, for loans advanced by other members of the same community, is strangely misconceived to constitute a debt contracted by the Government representing the whole community, and as such, has very erroneously figured in the imagination of all, who have treated of the Funding System, of its consequences, and of the remedy best fitted to repel the evils it inflicts, as impoverishing the country to the extent of the revenue raised.

Whilst to those, of whose minds this view of the subject has got possession, the community at once appears to exist in the character of a debtor, and though there is no person possessed of detached interests qualified to figure in the character of a

creditor, that difficulty is got the better of by a farther effort of imagination, which at once deputes to
that portion of the community which receives the
share of revenue paid in the shape of dividend, to
which they themselves have in part contributed,
the duty of playing the part of public creditors, and
strangely disclaims their receipts, as forming any
share of public wealth, though it is as much the
produce of the industry of the community as any
other part of it, and as such pays to Government for
protection, in the same manner as all other portions
of the property of the community.

The moment all these difficulties in establishing
the prevalent idea that the Funding System involves
the country in a debt, similar to that which a private
individual contracts by extravagance, are thus got
rid of by the aid of habitual misapplication of language, and of constant recourse to false analogies,
the advocates of the system seem not only to consider their reasoning plain and intelligible, but it is
advanced with a degree of confidence which leads to
the presumption that they deem it unanswerable :
the Government representing the public is freely
talked of as deeply involved in debt, and the annuity paid in the shape of dividend is considered as
a burden, which, in proportion to its extent, impoverishes the community at large, and disqualifies
it for future exertion.

The Committee of Finance, for example, make no
scruple in asserting " that a nation is bound, on the
" return of peace to make every effort to reduce

" the charge that has arisen from a system of bor-
" rowing during war; declaring that it requires no
" argument to prove that a course of policy founded
" upon the avowed principle of raising loans for
" the exigencies of a state in time of war, and of
" making no provision for diminishing the charges of
" those loans in time of peace, is an abandonment
" of all consideration for the credit and safety of the
" country, and a line of conduct, which makes it
" certain that the fabric of public credit must
" crumble under accumulated pressure."

Thus obviously avowing the opinion, which they deem so self-evident as to require no argument, that the revenue of a community, like that of an individual, may not only be impaired, but even exhausted by extraordinary expenditure, and that it can only be recruited by a parsimonious application of a part of the revenue, withdrawn from expenditure, and accumulated into capital by the force of legislative enactment.

In my last letter, I contended against the inferences drawn from the analogies of private life, in so far as they went to establish the principle that borrowing in the time of war, in the manner now practised for upwards of a century in this country, had the effect of impoverishing the community, arguing that the sole result of such an operation was altering the distribution of property amongst the various individuals belonging to the community, the aggregate of which forms the mass of national wealth, and also contending that a Sinking Fund, so far from counteracting that evil, was the means of all others the most active in aggravating it.

But the opinions I have quoted, as stated by this Committee to be self-evident, and to require in their estimation no argument, compel me to go a little further, and to explain to you and the public the grounds, on which I am disposed distinctly and confidently to contend, that the additional inferences from the analogies of private life, by which it is attempted to create an impression that parsimony or abstinence from expenditure, enforced by legislative restraint, (the principle on which all Sinking Funds proceed,) is a means of enriching a community—are as unfounded as that reasoning which goes to establish, that contracting a public debt (as it is called) impoverishes and diminishes the resources of a community; for in direct contradiction to these opinions I mean to maintain, and I think I shall succeed in convincing every reasonable man, that theory and experience co-operate in enforcing the opinion that the extravagant expenditure, to which the Funding System has enabled this country to have recourse in time of war, has had a direct tendency both to increase its wealth and its population ; and that, on the other hand, abstinence from expenditure and accumulation into capital of a part of the revenue of a country, which forms the means the advocates of a Sinking Fund contemplate of increasing the resources of a country, is of all others the policy best calculated to impoverish, and ultimately to discourage the increase of population in any community, who seriously persevere in the practice.

Before however I attempt by argument to justify these opinions, so directly opposite to those generally maintained, and so contradictory of those, on which the Committee of Finance have in their Report proceeded, I am confident you will agree with me in thinking we have had in our time so much experience of great extra expenditure during war, that it is expedient to examine, whether the result exhibits what must have inevitably taken place, if there is any foundation for the opinion, which the Committee think self-evident, that the resources of a country must be impaired and ultimately annihilated by a continuance of extravagant expenditure, the means of which is derived from mortgaging our revenue; or whether, in point of fact, the experience of what has really taken place does not strongly countenance the opinion, which I am about to maintain, that this is a means of increasing the collective wealth of a community; for after all, the inferences authorised by experience on such subjects may be rested upon as so much more conclusive than those which are founded upon general reasoning, that, unless my speculations received countenance from the former, I should feel too suspicious of the justice of the latter to press either on you or the public any conclusions that stood exclusively upon such grounds.

On our past experience of the effects of war-expenditure in enriching a community, I have, in my last Letter, already appealed with confidence to the observation of every man, who looked around him, and saw the universal change denoting unusual rapid increase of wealth in all ranks and conditions of life, during the progress of the most expensive war in which any country ever was engaged; but in confirmation of what I have stated, and to prove to the world that I have not been led by any love of theory to exaggerate the rapid progress of our wealth, during the period of the last war, I beg to refer you to the testimony of a man, whose many amiable qualities must always command my respect, but who lived and died a uniform supporter of those opinions on the subject of the Sinking Fund, on which the Committeee in their Report have relied.

The late Earl of Liverpool, in the year 1822—in a speech which I would not quote, had he not himself given to the public a corrected edition of it—after shewing the great increase of population that had taken place during the years of warfare, the most expensive (which is, in truth, only a natural consequence of an extraordinary demand for labour), and after stating that it is universally admitted, and that indeed there was an immense mass of evidence to prove, that agriculture, no less than manufactures and commerce, was in a most thriving state in this country during the latter years of the last war, proceeds to draw a direct comparison betwixt the wealth of the country in the year 1792, previous to the war with France, and the wealth of the country at the conclusion of it, in the following terms:—

" If we look at the commerce and wealth of this

" country at the present moment, and compare them
" with its commerce and wealth previous to the year
" 1792, we cannot for a moment doubt the ability of
" the country to bear the increased taxation which
" has taken place since that time. There are few of
" your Lordships who recollect the circumstances
" of the period to which I refer. There are fewer
" still, who, having participated in the discussions
" which took place at that period on the various
" financial and political interests of the country, are
" thereby enabled to calculate and appreciate the
" present condition of all the branches of the national
" industry, as compared with their condition antece-
" dent to the French Revolution. But, my Lords,
" we have documents on the subject, which cannot
" deceive us. Those documents will show what the
" real state of the country was at that period, as
" compared with its present condition. They will
" show how large a part of the present wealth of the
" country has accumulated since, and is absolutely a
" new creation. This fact is so undeniable, that any
" man who lived in this country prior to the year 1792,
" and who, having been absent from it ever since,
" were now to revisit it for the first time, would
" find the whole face of the country entirely altered.

" I will take the average return of the exports and
" imports for the three years antecedent to the year
" 1790, and the average returns for the last three
" years. The average amount calculated at their
" official value, of British manufactures exported
" during the three years, ending the 5th of January
" 1787, the 5th of January 1788, and the 5th of

" January 1789, was 12,852,780*l.* The average
" amount exported during the three years, ending
" the 5th of January 1819, the 5th of January 1820,
" and the 5th of January 1821 (a period including,
" as your Lordships will observe, an unfavourable
" year—that of 1820) was 40,146,245*l.* The average
" amount of imports for the three years, ending the
" 5th of January 1787, the 5th of January 1788, and
" the 5th of January 1789, was 17,884,104*l.* The
" average amount for three years, ending the 5th of
" January 1819, the 5th of January 1820, and the
" 5th of January 1821, was 36,759,650*l.* Here
" there is an incontrovertible proof that in the pe-
" riod which has elapsed since the commencement
" of the last war, our exports have been more than
" trebled; that they have been nearly quadrupled;
" and that our imports have been nearly trebled.

" If, my Lords, we also take into our consideration
" the other branches of our industry, inseparably
" connected with the prosperity of our commerce,
" and the produce of which has not only kept pace
" with the great increase of our population, but has
" very much surpassed it, we shall feel that the
" question as to the great increase of the wealth
" of the country since the year 1792, notwithstand-
" ing the mighty exertions, which, in the interval,
" we have been compelled to make, is completely
" set at rest.

" Adverting now to the state of agriculture, it
" cannot be necessary to remind your Lordships of
" the vast number of Enclosure Bills which have

" passed since the year 1792. Indeed, every man's
" observation, in passing from one part of the country
" to another, must be sufficient to convince him of
" the great and favourable change which has taken
" place in that respect. Whole districts and im-
" mense tracts of hitherto unproductive lands have
" been broken up and tilled. In whatever direction
" we travel; whether we go the north, to the south,
" or to the west, we find what were formerly dreary
" wastes and commons, and sheep-walks, now
" brought into cultivation. I admit that, in many
" instances, this has been a forced operation; but
" what an augmentation has it occasioned of public
" and individual wealth! Let your Lordships also
" consider the state of the old lands, which were in
" cultivation before the period to which I have
" alluded; how greatly they have been improved,
" and how considerably their rents have been ad-
" vanced, continuing even at this moment of depres-
" sion, far above the scale of 1792, notwithstanding
" the recent reductions, which, I confess, I think it
" a great misfortune were not made sooner. All
" these facts prove the great increase of agricultural
" wealth."

He then proceeds at great length to show how a
similar augmentation had taken place in the production of all articles subject to excise duties, stating
in detail the unparalleled increase, during the war, in
the consumption of tea, candles, soap, leather, and
of all those things, which contribute not merely to
the enjoyment of those possessed of overgrown

wealth, but of articles, the great and increasing abundance of which afford the best proof that the community at large, from its increasing wealth, had the means of acquiring, and have actually enjoyed a more extensive supply of what from habit form the comforts of life, than they ever antecedently enjoyed ; and in the conclusion of this speech, which is far more valuable for its admissions, than even for its extensive information, he, in a manner the most convincing, assigns his reasons for thinking that the war expenditure was the occasion of that great and increasing production, the particulars of which he had on the evidence of official documents detailed.

And that he was right in the cause he assigned for this great augmentation in the production and consumption of commodities—which is the only sure proof of a community's enjoying increased wealth— cannot be disputed, unless some of our modern economical quacks can so mislead the public mind as to make it forget the sound principle, which, in economical reasoning, never for a moment ought to be lost sight of, that an augmentation of demand is sure to increase the exchangeable value of all com- modities, and that, as long as the nature of man remains unaltered, such an increase cannot take place, without calling forth more active and extended exertions of industry, by which means alone the wealth and resources of a country—which is always great in proportion to the extent of its production— can be increased.

Important, however, as these admissions must appear when made by a man, who, more than any other, had opportunities of information, as evidence of the fact, that the greatest war expenditure that any country ever sustained, had not the effects ascribed to it by the Finance Committee, of either diminishing the resources, or reducing the wealth of the community, it is certain that there are more solid proofs of this important fact, than that which is acquired by relying on the testimony of Lord Liverpool, or that of any other man.

Those, who recollect that the whole amount of capital, with difficulty raised by loan for the public service, in the years 1793 and 1794 (the two first years of our war with France) was under fifteen millions, and who witnessed the commercial difficulties, that this comparatively feeble exertion occasioned,— which was such as to render it necessary for Government to interfere, by advancing money to sustain the credit of individuals in nearly two hundred and thirty-eight cases, and that to the extent of upwards of two millions,—have only to reflect that, in the last three years of our long protracted warfare, (that is, in the years 1813, 1814 and 1815) there was raised for the public service, beside what was applicable to the National Debt, the sum of three hundred and three millions,—the three years at the end of the war, in which Lord Liverpool announces that the agriculture, manufactures, and commerce of the country were in the most thriving possible state; for that fact of itself affords conclusive evidence that the largest war expenditure ever known, instead of abridging the resources and impairing the wealth of the community, proved to be the most rapid means of adding to the public wealth, and of course of increasing those resources, which if it is necessary for its protection, the community can at all times command.

Such are the facts established by the clearest documentary evidence, in part detailed by a Minister who cannot be deemed a willing witness to anything, which makes the supposed benefits to be derived from a Sinking Fund questionable; for he concludes this very speech by declaring that he deems the steady maintenance of an efficient Sinking Fund a principle so indispensable, that upon it he is determined to rise or fall.

Yet it cannot be denied that these details—so far from justifying the conclusion which the Committee of Finance assumes to be so self-evident as to require no support from argument—prove, beyond the possibility of doubt, that, in the course of twenty-four years of almost continued warfare, during which the funding system was resorted to for the means of defraying our expenditure, to an extent unparalleled, the wealth of the country increased, and its resources became extensive to a degree unexampled.

Having thus established the important fact, that a great war expenditure, maintained by the system we have in this country so long practised, has proved itself the means of adding to the wealth and resources of the country, I might next proceed to call your attention to the reasoning on general principles, which, in my opinion, decidedly proves that this must be the result of all extra expenditure, the means of defraying which is acquired by funding ; a proposition which I conceive may be made as evident, as the fact of our wealth having increased during the late war has been made apparent.

On reflection, however, I prefer canvassing, in the first place, what symptoms are to be discovered of the wealth of the community having increased, by the application of that surplus of revenue over expenditure, to the extent of 20,753,545*l.* which the Committee state to have been the total amount of the surplus applicable to the diminution of our debt, in the twelve years which succeeded the termination of the late war ; though a larger sum arising from balances unappropriated in the Exchequer has been applied to that purpose, amounting in all to 31,990,369*l.* For on this subject I am also free to confess, that, if I found, on examination, that the fact sustained the opinion the Committee have so confidently pronounced, and that there existed symptoms of increased wealth, indicating an extension of our resources, as the result of this arrangement, I have so much more respect for the conclusions justified by experience, than for those which are derived from general reasoning, that I should at once abstain from pressing you, or any public man, to act on any opinion which could not be maintained on the former ground, though I must always feel more confident of the rectitude of my opinion, when theory and experience appear to unite in establishing the justice of it.

I will therefore now proceed to consider what

symptoms can be discovered of our resources being extended, or the wealth of the community having increased, in consequence of that expenditure in the shape of a real Sinking Fund since the peace, which to the Committee has appeared to be—the only mode of recruiting what they are pleased to describe as our exhausted resources, and the sure means of augmenting the wealth of the community : after which I will endeavour, as shortly as possible, to explain the general principles which lead me to maintain that a great extraordinary expenditure, beyond the amount of the revenue of a community, must always encrease its wealth—and, on the other hand, to assign the reasoning that makes me regard abstinence from expenditure, or parsimony ; (that is, expending less than the produce of the revenue, for the purpose of increasing the general amount of capital,) as a certain means of diminishing the public wealth of every community.

Now, in endeavouring to ascertain the mere fact, whether there are any symptoms of the public wealth of this country having been augmented, or our resources increased by the application to the redemption of (what is called) our debt, of the sum of 20,753,545*l.* which the Committee state to be the amount of surplus revenue, so applied, or even by the application of the larger sum of 31,990,369*l.* arising from balances in the Exchequer, which have been gradually brought to account and conjoined with that surplus, I might again appeal to the reasonings and details of Lord Liverpool, in the studied dissertation he published on the state of the nation, which, from beginning to end, can only lead to the conclusion that the Committee have formed a very erroneous opinion, when they represent this proceeding as having augmented either the wealth or the resources of the Community.

But to decide the question it is unnecessary to appeal to the statement of any individual, however great his authority; for, if public wealth has been truly defined to be the aggregate of the wealth of all the individuals of whom the community consists, it could not receive any addition without perceptibly increasing the wealth of some of our fellow-subjects. There is unfortunately, however, no class of the community whose evidence would not impeach the accuracy of the opinion, the Committee has so confidently pronounced to be self-evident.

Ask the landholder; he will inform you that, though undoubtedly, since the peace, he has had it in his power to borrow at a lower rate of interest, still the permanent diminution of his rental, and in many cases partial abatements, which the times have rendered necessary, have greatly reduced his revenue, notwithstanding of which his reduced rents have been collected with greater difficulty than during the war, when the returns from his property were much larger, though we were annually raising by the funding system sums unparalleled in extent.

Ask the farmer; and, though he will be obliged to confess that the sense of equity, which has always guided the conduct of the landholders of this country, has greatly reduced the rent he pays, yet he must inform you that the times have been such, and the diminution in the price of his produce so great, that though he has curtailed his expenditure, even to the extent of depriving himself and his family of those comforts they were habitually accustomed to enjoy, yet the capital he had amassed during the war has been nearly exhausted by the calls he has been compelled to make on it, to pay the reduced rents, with which he has been charged. And, if any one can doubt that the change in the state of agricultural labour during this period, indicates a diminution and not an increase in the wealth of those who are employed in executing it, he has only to look at the various Reports on the Corn Laws, and the state of the Corn Trade, where he will find evidence of the general reduction of wages and the increase of Poor-rates, which cannot fail to convince him that, since the war, that industrious class of the community, from whose labour we derive our food, have shared the fate of the farmer and of his landlord.

If, on the other hand, you ask the master manufacturer, or the operative in manufacturing labour, whether, since the cessation of the war expenditure, they have experienced any increase of their wealth, which, in making up the general account of the aggregate of national wealth, could authorise the supposition that any augmentation could be derived from that quarter, the answer I am afraid would be melancholy.

The former must tell you that, although, from the great reduction of price, which if not counteracted by other circumstances must always increase the number of consumers of every commodity, and, of course, the demand for it, aided by the temporary demand arising from goods purchased with a view to convey capital abroad, to be invested in foreign loans, as well as by speculations founded on the probable demand from the New South American States, which, for a time, was carried to a ruinous extent; he has been enabled to keep his establishment a going, yet he has acquired little or no profit, and has only done so from thinking that, if he had suddenly withdrawn from business and abandoned all hope of future profit from the share of his capital invested in houses, machinery, and implements necessary for the conduct of the concern, his loss would have been still greater.

Whilst from the latter, truth can only admit of a statement that at a rate of wages greatly reduced, he has generally, though not always, been able to procure scanty employment, but that he still looks back with regret for the loss of those times of great expenditure, before we began to attempt enriching ourselves by forcing, through legislative enactment, a portion of our revenue to be withdrawn from expenditure, for the purpose of converting it into capital; when he recollects having constant employment at wages to the extent, in many instances, of more than double the amount of what he has since enjoyed.

Again, ask the merchant and the banker; and they must inform you that their profits are reduced to a degree, that, if they could have anticipated what has taken place, since recourse was had to this plan of an efficient Sinking Fund for enriching the community, they would long ago have retired from business; and no man can doubt the truth of their assertion, who reflects upon the great losses, which that melancholy record of bankruptcies since exhibited in the Gazette, must have inflicted on the trading and monied interest throughout the community.

But of the fact, that our public wealth has not increased during this period, the strongest of all proof is to be derived from the unparalleled number of petitions, stating the distress that has alternately prevailed in every branch of industry, as well as from the numerous experiments made by the legislature to restore that feeling of content, which always attends generally increasing wealth, and which certainly prevailed during the war; that is, at the time our resources, according to the Committee, were diminishing to a ruinous extent.

No one, who has attended to the proceedings in Parliament, can fail to recollect that the sufferings of those engaged in agricultural industry, who enjoyed unexampled prosperity during our extraordinary expenditure, first attracted the attention of Government on the return of peace.

Agriculture was then represented as the most important branch of our national industry; the soil of these kingdoms, with due encouragement, was, except in seasons of extraordinary sterility, deemed adequate to produce a sufficiency for the nourishment of our increased and increasing population;

and to secure an augmented supply, there was given to this branch of industry a more formidable protection against foreign competition, than it had enjoyed under any law passed since the times of King Charles the Second, and King William the Third. The remedy, however, seems not to have produced the desired effect of restoring the prosperity that this species of industry had enjoyed during the time, that, in the opinion of the Committee, we were destroying our resources and impairing the national wealth; it succeeded however in generating complaints on the part of the merchants and manufacturers, who remonstrated against the measure as inflicting great hardship on them; whilst the agriculturists themselves began, by petitions, so loudly to express their sufferings, under what they represented to be a law which afforded inadequate and inefficacious relief, that further enquiries were deemed necessary, which ended in a Report condemning almost every system, and terminating, after more than hinting that superabundance of production was the real cause of the evil, with a most unsatisfactory declaration that, after a long and anxious enquiry, the Committee were unable to discover any means, which, in their estimation, were calculated immediately to relieve the present pressure.

This, however, was the prelude to complaints arising from almost all quarters against the existing system of law, by which the agricultural interest was protected; and our Government, who but a few years before had loudly proclaimed that superabundant production was the cause of the complaints of the agriculturist, gradually talked themselves into a conviction that, without foreign supply, the population of this country could not be ensured in a sufficiency of food; and into a belief that, whilst the corn imported from abroad would enrich the community, by creating a fresh demand for our manufactures, the reduced price of food would produce a similar effect. And thus, on a principle directly the reverse of that on which they had at first proceeded, in relation to agricultural produce, they resolved to attempt restoring the feeling of general satisfaction, that always attends increasing wealth, by admitting foreigners, under certain limitations, to a share in supplying us with food.

How this new experiment will succeed, remains to be proved; at present the country has not had sufficient experience to form a distinct opinion of its effects, though it is certain that neither the grower nor the consumer of grain express much satisfaction, and that hitherto it seems to afford most benefit to the speculators.

These short details are not stated with a view to criticize the conduct of those with whom these various measures originated; but to shew that, during the time we have been attempting to increase our wealth, by accumulating into capital a real surplus of revenue, we have been driven from one experiment to another by loud, perhaps irresistible, complaints of poverty and distress; and that all have alike failed in restoring that feeling of content and prosperity we enjoyed, when, in the opinion of the Committee, we were pursuing a line of conduct ruinous to our resources, and destructive of our national prosperity.

To go as much at large into all the various experiments that have been made on other branches of industry, urged on by similar complaints of distress, and which have all, more or less, failed of success, would lead to a detail unnecessary ; for they are only here alluded to as proofs that this abstinence from expenditure, and recourse to parsimony, which the Committee so confidently recommend, has not produced the general feeling of content which always attends increasing public wealth.

It is sufficient therefore to preface a short enumeration of them, by observing, what cannot be denied, that during this period there is no branch of industry from which we have not had complaints of distress, and with regard to which we have not made ineffectual efforts to afford relief, by experiments that have uniformly done more injury to other branches of industry, than they have done good to those they were intended to benefit.

Passing over the symptoms of discontent, arising from poverty, exhibited throughout all our manufacturing districts at the commencement of this period ; which perhaps, by the mistaken zeal of some, certainly by the mischievous arts and designs of others, were fostered into scenes bordering upon sedition, which we endeavoured to suppress by harsh legislative enactments, in contempt of the ever-memorable maxim of Lord Bacon, " that, on such occasions, " the first remedy or prevention is, to remove by all " means possible, want and poverty, the material " cause of sedition." We have since witnessed an attempt to relieve the distress of the woollen cloth manufactures, by repealing the duties on foreign wool, that has given rise to sufferings on the part of the wool grower, even to the extent of depriving them of all sale for the commodity, in raising which their capital had been embarked on the faith of long existing laws.

Again, we have seen an experiment to relieve the acknowledged general distress of our manufacturers, by breaking in upon that system of navigation laws so long the object of our admiration, recommended on the ground, that the cheaper the rate of freight for importing the raw material used in our manufactures, and the lower we paid for conveying them abroad, the cheaper we could bring them to the market; and inferring that this reduction of price was sure to increase the demand, and that the increased quantity sold must inevitably augment our public wealth; a scheme which has been productive of doubtful benefit to the manufacturers, and of vehement complaints on the part of the shipping interest.

Lastly, In indulging in this vein of experiment to relieve the distress so generally complained of, which, in the nature of things, could not have existed, had the wealth of the community been increasing, some of our statesmen, eager for popular reputation, have assumed to themselves the merit of introducing a system of free trade into this country, which they must know they never attempted; for the utmost the measures proposed announced, was an attempt to substitute prohibitory duties for prohibition; an arrangement which obviously could produce no good effect if the duties substituted were really prohibitory; and if they were not, was sure, under the circumstances of this country, whose capital is embarked on the faith of long subsisting legal enactments, unjustly to inflict great and serious injury on many branches of industry, in the conduct of which it was invested.

Be this as it may, there certainly can be no stronger proof of the existence of distress, which never prevails, when the wealth of a country is increasing, than these uniform scenes of complaint, and this attempt to acquire reputation, under pretence of introducing a system, which, however beneficial to the world at large, is thoroughly inapplicable to the state of this country; for, if those, who are said to assume the merit of doing what they never dared to attempt, know anything, they cannot doubt that freedom of trade, if it was enacted, would, in practice, prove the most ruinous system of restraint that could be introduced into a country such as this, possessing an immense capital embarked in various branches of industry, in the manner, in which individuals consulting their interest, thought most advantageous under that arrangement of our industry which our laws and our habits have long sanctioned.

Indeed even the slight approach towards *it* that has been made, by shifting the defences of our domestic industry from prohibition to prohibitory duties, has proved ruinous to some branches of our manufactures, whilst it has conferred but slight advantage on those it was supposed to have benefited ; furnishing proof most conclusive that general principles, however right in themselves, and however sound the conclusions to be derived from them when applied to the regulation of new states, whose industry is in its infancy, cannot, without mischievous results, be introduced into countries, where the distribution of property, and the existing laws, have long regulated the application both of the skill and the capital of the community.

I have entered into this detail, because I know not whether the loud and continued complaints of our manufacturers, or the numerous and shifting schemes for their relief, afford the strongest proof of that distress, which never could have been felt, if the system the Committee have recommended for increasing the wealth and resources of the community, and for which purpose they have reported a sum of 31,990,369*l*. to have been applied, had produced the expected effect.

Before quitting this branch of the subject, allow me to refer you to a Petition, which I printed for private circulation in the year 1820, when the proposal was made for a new arrangement of the Sinking Fund, by instituting a real efficient Sinking Fund of five millions, arising out of the surplus revenue we were then supposed to possess, with the addition of three millions to be raised by taxes then imposed, which will shew you that at that time, I perfectly agreed with Lord Liverpool in the effects he attributed to our war expenditure, whilst it will prove that I then regarded the Sinking Fund as sure to produce the effects we have since experienced from it, and which I am now more than ever inclined to believe must be the inevitable result of such an establishment.*

Having now stated the grounds, on which I think it impossible to deny that, in point of fact, the wealth of the country, as well as its population rapidly increased, during our late great war extra-expenditure, which the Committee have regarded as the means of diminishing our wealth, and impairing our resources; as well as the facts, which seem decidedly to prove that the public wealth, consisting of the aggregate of all the wealth possessed by the members of the community, has been impaired since we pursued the course of applying a real surplus to redeem what has been denominated our debt, which the Committee have announced to be, in their opinion, the only means of recruiting our resources;—and having endeavoured to prove to you that this is no new opinion on the effects which our past conduct has had on the state of our public wealth, by shew-

---

* The Petition forms the sole article in the Appendix to these Letters.

ing you that the sentiments expressed by Lord Liverpool—the complaints of those engaged in every branch of industry—the variety of novel experiments with doubtful effect—as well as the statement contained in the Petition I have given at length in the Appendix, all concur in establishing the fact that the community never expressed any feeling of distress during the time of our great extra expenditure; and that the feeling of universal distress, which is the surest symptom of decreasing wealth, has existed (with the exception of short intervals that might easily be accounted for) ever since we began to recruit our resources, by that line of conduct, which the Committee recommend as the only means of increasing public wealth.

It remains for me only to detail the reasoning which leads to the conclusion, that though productive of great and injurious alterations in the distribution of property, yet great extra expenditure for the maintenance of a war must always augment the wealth of a community; and the grounds, on which it appears to me impossible to deny that a system of forcibly abstracting a part of the revenue from expenditure, and accumulating it into capital, whilst it must occasion a similar mischievous alteration in the distribution of property, must unfortunately produce a diminution of the public wealth of a community.

Before however going into minute explanations of the mode in which extraordinary expenditure, by creating a demand for the produce of the industry of a community, must always increase its wealth, and of the mode in which abstinence from expenditure, by diminishing the demand for the produce of the industry of a community, must always produce the contrary effect, there is one mode of considering the question, which I cannot refrain from stating, because I think it is alone sufficient to prove the erroneous view of the subject the Committee entertain, when they regard extra expenditure as a means of impoverishing a community, and parsimony, or abstinence from expenditure, as the means of recruiting its resources.

If abstinence from expenditure, and accumulation of that part of the revenue assumed by taxation to the extent of five millions, is really a means of bestowing so great a benefit as that of increasing the wealth of a community, it would be difficult to imagine why a proceeding productive of a result so universally beneficial should be limited to so small a sum ; for, if it is really a means of increasing public wealth, it seems to follow that the further a system is pushed, productive of such eminent advantage, the greater will be the extent of the benefit insured to the community.

But if, in this country, the legislature was, by a sumptuary law, to force every individual in the community to abstain from expending the value of one half of what his industry, his land, or his property, however vested, produced, and to accumulate it into capital; or, what is the same thing in as far as the collective wealth of the community is concerned, if the legislature was to raise the one half of the revenue by taxation, and to transfer it to Commissioners for the purpose of laying it out as capital, the ruin, to which such a proceeding would immediately give rise, must be apparent.

It is obvious the demand for the produce of the industry of a country, in which such a measure was resorted to, must at once be reduced one half; there would remain therefore a surplus to that extent in the hands of the grower or the manufacturer; and, if it has been truly laid down, for which authorities innumerable might be cited, that the existence of one-tenth more of a commodity than what is consumed, would reduce its market value one half, it must be apparent that the existence of one half more than is consumed, would place a community in a state, concerning which fortunately there is no experience that can lead us to any accurate conclusion, though there is undoubtedly no reasonable being who must not admit it to be self-evident that, far from insuring an increase of wealth, it would occasion thorough and complete ruin.

It must therefore be evident, even to those who are most sanguine in their ideas of parsimony, as a means of recruiting the resources, and extending the wealth of a community, that there are bounds to the extent to which the system can be carried; and yet it seems impossible to state any reason that can justify the opinion that a measure which, if pushed to the extent of one half of the revenue of a community, must be completely ruinous, should become the only means of increasing the wealth of a community, if it is limited to the sum of three, five, or ten millions.

We have had experience in this country of an extra expenditure to the extent of three hundred millions in the course of three years, at the termination of twenty years, during which an extra expenditure, unparalleled in the records of history, took place; yet proofs have been adduced, and that undeniable, that we sustained no inconvenience, and that there is no period of our history when all classes of the community enjoyed greater prosperity; or when the face of the country exhibited generally stronger proofs of increased and increasing wealth.

Now, without having recourse to a supposition so extravagant as that of the legislature's withdrawing one half of the demand for the whole produce of the country, let us suppose that we had, by legislative enactment, for three years withdrawn from expenditure one hundred millions in each year, and left the commodities, for which a demand would have existed to that extent in the hands of those who produced them, can any one doubt that, by such a measure, the industrious part of the community must have been involved in a state of misery such as no community ever endured?

But, if we have had experience of the legislature's having authorised an extra expenditure to the extent of three hundred millions in the course of three years, during which time all the various branches of industry in the country appeared to those, who had the best opportunity of information, to be in a most flourishing state, and, if it is impossible to conceive that we should not have been involved in ruin by a legislative enactment, enforcing the necessity of saving to the same amount, it seems difficult to understand upon what ground the Committee can maintain, that great extraordinary expenditure diminishes the wealth of a country, and that abstinence from expenditure increases it.

The fair conclusion, which seems irresistibly to press upon us from this view of the subject, is in itself very different; for as parsimony appears obviously ruinous, when pushed to such an extreme, it is much more natural to infer that a diminution of the extent, to which it is carried, rendering the injury less marked and material, the effects of it become less perceptible, than to infer that abridging the amount of the sum saved and accumulated, should so completely change the character of the measure as to render it the only means of increasing wealth.

But to bring this discussion to a conclusion, by shewing, as shortly and as clearly as possible, how parsimony must always diminish the public or collective wealth of every community, and how extra expenditure must always have the contrary effect of increasing it, allow me to state some general propositions, which appear such as may be assumed without the dread of controversy.

1st. It can hardly be disputed, that wealth may be defined as consisting of what man desires as useful or delightful to him; nor can it be doubted that, as the enjoyment of these things in increasing abundance must establish the fact of an increase of wealth, so a diminution in the quantity must be considered as evidence of the decrease of wealth.

2dly. It may with certainty be assumed that, in a country such as this, advanced to a high state of civilization and improvement, the share of the objects of man's desire, which he derives from the direct gift of nature, is small, and of itself unsusceptible of increase; that it is therefore from the exertions of their industry that the members of such a community derive infinitely the greatest portion of the objects of their desire, and that a steady perseverance in their attempts to increase these exertions, forms the sole and the unlimited means of augmenting the wealth of a community.

From these two simple and incontrovertible propositions, it plainly and distinctly follows, that in judging of the effects of the measures of a legislature or of a Government, with a view to decide whether they tend to enrich or to impoverish a country, the only course that can be pursued, which promises to guide the mind to an accurate conclusion, is to examine, whether they tend to encourage or discourage the general exertions of industry throughout the community. For in the degree they encourage such exertions, wealth must increase, as certainly as it must decrease in the proportion they tend to discourage it.

But, if this inference from these two plain, and as

they appear to me incontrovertible propositions, is just and accurate, the solution of the important questions,—whether parsimony is most accurately described when predicated to be a means of recruiting our resources, and of increasing our wealth,—or when stated to be a means of diminishing it,—and whether extra expenditure tends to enrich or impoverish a country, lies within a very narrow compass, and certainly requires neither extended discussion nor elaborate argument.

Indeed, I have always thought, that it was to vague and often inapplicable analogies and illustrations, and to ingenious reasoning founded on such premises—often resorted to by men who felt conscious that, in this subject, they themselves laboured under doubt and hesitation—to which the delusion so generally prevalent ought to be ascribed; and prepossessions thus created are certainly best repelled by plain, short, and direct statements, which seem at once to be the means most efficient of dispelling fallacies thus established, and of impressing a permanent conviction of the accuracy of those views, which accord with truth.

First then, I submit that diminution of expenditure in every community must diminish the demand for its produce, whilst extra expenditure in every community must increase the demand for it, and that a diminution of demand must always, in the nature of things, diminish the price of commodities, and an augmentation of demand increase it.

Secondly, It is with equal confidence I assume,—
that a diminution of the price of commodities is a
sure means of diminishing the exertions of industry
applied to the production of them ;—that an increase
of the price of commodities is a certain means of
calling forth additional exertions of industry in producing them ;—and that the greater the exertions of
industry in any community, the greater must be the
quantity of its produce.

Assuming these propositions to be established,
which have never yet been doubted, either by practical men or by theorists, it follows that, if it could
be further assumed—that a diminution of the annual
produce of a community is in truth a diminution
of its wealth,—and that an increase of the annual
produce of a community, and an increase of its
wealth, are one and the same thing, it would become
impossible to doubt that a diminution of expenditure
and an increase of expenditure must produce the
same effects which experience shews they have
heretofore uniformly produced ;—the first in impoverishing, and the last in enriching every community
where it takes place.

But this, although it appears evidently as correct
as any of the propositions I have previously,
without hesitation, submitted as indisputable, cannot be assumed ; for it is the strange and singular
opinion that capital exclusively constitutes wealth,
and that an increase of capital is therefore the only
means of increasing it, which forms the foundation

of the doctrine that has been so universally received, and which is now sanctioned by the Committee, who assume as a thing not to be doubted, that expenditure diminishes the mass of our national resources, and of our national wealth, and that parsimony is the only means of recruiting the one or of increasing the other.

That this is the view of the subject Mr Pitt entertained, and that his followers adopted, is undoubted; for, in that remarkable speech, which he afterwards published, and which Mr Canning in 1827 quoted, as containing his views in relation to the Sinking Fund, Mr Pitt states Dr Smith to be the first person who had accurately developed and explained the nature of capital, and the effects of the accumulation thereof; and it is certain that a person who boasted coincidence of opinion with the author of the Wealth of Nations on this subject, must, in consistency, have maintained that increasing capital was exclusively the means of augmenting wealth.

For those who are acquainted with the works of that excellent man, must be aware that, although he ridicules the folly of accumulating circulating capital, (which is a necessary preliminary to the accumulation by parsimony of capital of any description) comparing it to the amassing of a number of pots and pans more than are necessary; yet, with a singular degree of inconsistency, he considers parsimony to be the only means of increasing wealth, maintaining, that wealth is increased by parsimony and not by industry,*—that every prodigal is a public enemy, and every frugal man a public benefactor,†—that labour is exclusively put in motion by capital,‡—that labour, or exertions of industry, are always dependant on the amount of capital,‖—and that the general industry of a country is always proportioned to the capital which employs it.§ Opinions which, if true, would render it impossible even for those who look to additional exertions of industry as the sole means of augmenting wealth, to say that an augmentation of capital was not a necessary preliminary; for, if capital so completely regulated the exertions of industry that, without it was increased, no additional exertions of industry could take place in any community, it would undoubtedly follow that an increase of capital must be regarded as exclusively the means of increasing wealth.

But Dr Smith wrote at a time, when the origin of the profit of capital had not been developed or explained. Had he been aware of what is now generally admitted, that the profit of all capital arises from its performing a portion of labour that would otherwise be performed by the hand of man, or from its executing a portion of labour beyond the reach of

---

* Volume II, page 137.   ‖ Volume I, page 3.
† Volume I, page 414.   § Volume II, page 37.
‡ Volume I, pages 437, 441, 445.

the power of man to accomplish, he would not have been misled into the beaten track, which Turgot and others of the French philosophers had pursued, which leads to the erroneous conclusion that parsimony is to be regarded as the sole means of increasing public wealth.

For the moment the nature of capital is understood—the duties it performs in all its branches, whether fixed or circulating, defined—and the means by which it secures a profit are explained and made evident, the idea must vanish that it may with benefit be increased to an indefinite extent, always augmenting the wealth of the community in proportion as it is augmented.

As it then becomes obvious that its value must be fixed on the same general principle with the value of every other commodity, and it is at once apparent that you cannot increase the quantity, without diminishing the market rate of profits that it secures, which must affect the rate of profit on the capital already existing, and that at a time when you are abstracting by taxation a sum of revenue which would otherwise be expended in consumable commodities, and which must of course abridge the demand for what the existing capital is employed in producing; for, as long as the nature of man remains unchanged, the knowledge of what has been consumed, and of the degree of avidity displayed in the market for the different articles of consumption, must imperiously regulate both the nature and quantity of what is subsequently produced.

The demand for capital—which is only useful for the purpose of performing labour in producing that which the community wants to consume—must therefore be diminished at the moment its amount is increased, and thus, at one and the same time, the existing capital of the country must be assailed by the only two efficient means by which the value of any commodity can be reduced; and it is impossible to deny that this must discourage all effort to increase it in the only mode in which capital and public wealth can be simultaneously increased.

I know it has been maintained, that saving out of the existing revenue is the only means of increasing capital; but there is no proposition more false and unfounded.

Capital, which is only useful to man for the purpose of executing labour, consists of a part of the produce of the earth, or a part of the earth itself, to which either nature or art has given a form that adapts it for the purpose of performing labour.

Now there are certainly two means of increasing this portion of the wealth of mankind.

1st. It may be increased by additional exertions of industry, directed to the production and formation of things every way useful to supplant and perform labour.

2ndly. It may be increased by abstracting a portion of labour employed in forming consumable commodities, and applying it to the formation of things every way useful in supplanting the necessity of and performing labour.

When augmented by the first of these means, it is obvious that capital and public wealth, if it is rightly defined to be the aggregate of all commodities, are proportionably augmented ; and it is equally clear that, when it is increased by the second of these means, capital and public wealth, or the aggregate of all commodities, are not augmented in the same proportion, for what is gained to the wealth of the community by the increase of capital, must be lost by the diminution of consumable commodities, which the abstraction from demand must occasion.

Nay more, if the abstraction from expenditure of a sum equal to what by parsimony is added to the capital of the community, causes a diminution of production to that extent, parsimony must be considered as a means of creating capital, at the expence of sacrificing a revenue as great as the capital created ; and it does not appear that a more ruinous operation in all its bearings can be devised than that of disposing of an annual income (for example, of a million) for the purpose of acquiring a capital to the same amount.

Yet that this must be the fate of every community, that attempts to increase its public wealth, by augmenting its capital at the expence of withdrawing the natural encouragement to production (which is the sure result of parsimony) is undoubted; unless the proposition is false, the truth of which is universally admitted, that the whole quantity of industry usually employed to bring commodities into the market for the consumption of the community, always suits itself to the existing demand ; for a community cannot add to its wealth by impoverishing the members of the community, though an individual can, and too often does add to his wealth by impoverishing his neighbours.

Perhaps a shorter process might have been pursued to produce a conviction, that it is not an enlargement of its capital, which in any community constitutes an augmentation of its wealth. For, as land, labour and capital, the sole sources of wealth, are alone useful or desirable in so far as they tend to produce that which satisfies the objects of men's desires (whether in administering to his sustenance or pleasing his taste) it must be apparent that an increase of any of these three sources of wealth, at the expence of diminishing that production, from contributing to the growth and formation of which they alone derive their value, cannot be a means of increasing the wealth of a community, and that it is therefore ridiculous to look to an increase of capital as a means of augmenting wealth, if it is to be effected by withdrawing that encouragement to the increase of production of what man desires as useful and delightful, which alone constitutes real wealth, and a diminution of which always must impoverish a community.

To execute the task I have undertaken, it only now remains for me to explain to you the grounds on which I have presumed to assert, that extra expenditure always must increase the wealth of every community, and this I might do within a very narrow compass; for, if I have been successful in convincing you of the evil which always must attend the legislative restraint in the management of property a Sinking Fund imposes, by blindly dictating the quantity of revenue, which should be withdrawn from expenditure and accumulated into capital, without any previous examination into the effects of either operation, it follows that extra expenditure, being the policy in every respect opposite to that which has been shown to impoverish a community, must produce the contrary effect—to wit, that of enriching a community.

But the question is too important to allow it to stand merely upon that inference, however conclusive.

Besides, the process by which it must produce this effect, may be shortly stated in a manner which puts it beyond all possibility of doubt.

That the revenue and expenditure of all countries must be equivalent, if left to the natural course of things, is a proposition so generally admitted, as to require no illustration; indeed, it is impossible that such a state of things should long exist, as any great variation between them ; for, if part of that produce, which constitutes the revenue of every country was not by expenditure consumed, it would form such a discouragement to future production, as, by diminishing the amount of it, would soon restore the equivalency; whilst, on the other hand, an extra expenditure, by giving encouragement to increased production, would very soon command the same result.

Now it is known to all, that the Funding System, by levying from some of the members of the community a share of their capital in exchange for the right of receiving the stipulated revenue out of the taxes imposed, which, in time of war, is expended in the purchase of what is deemed necessary for the protection of the whole community, must, by such extra expenditure, add to the demand which naturally would arise from the expenditure of the revenue, in a degree proportioned to the amount of the loan raised.

This must inevitably elevate the price of all commodities; and that advanced price not only enables the growers and manufacturers to expend more (which forms a further source of increased demand) but also to lay out a part of what they acquire by the extra price they receive for the produce of their industry, in the formation of things useful to supplant and perform labour, at a time when the increased and increasing consumption requires such aid to assist in supplying the market, by which means an increase of capital is acquired at the very moment the revenue of the industrious is increasing in consequence of the augmentation of demand, and not as parsimony attempts to increase capital by the inconsistent operation of diminishing the demand for what it can alone be profitably employed in producing.

Neither is it capital alone that is sure to be increased by this extra expenditure, for the extended demand for labour, to which it gives rise, of which only a share is performed by capital, must increase the wages of all labourers, whilst it gives to their children at an earlier period the power of maintaining themselves by labour, thus annihilating the moral check on matrimony, and of course increasing the population of the country.

To establish the accuracy of this short detail of the mode, in which extra expenditure during warfare, (the means of defraying which is acquired by funding), operates in increasing the collective wealth of a community, reference may be made to what has been already stated on the subject of the increased wages and profits, to which our experience has shewn it uniformly gave rise, as well as to the numerous complaints of distress for want of employment, occasioned by the diminution of demand for all the productions of our industry since our extra expenditure ceased, and since we have endeavoured by parsimony to abstract from expenditure, and to devote to accumulation, even a share of that, which, if left in the hands of the community, would have naturally been expended. It is certain too, that those, who recollect the exultation with which our increased and increasing population during the years of extra expenditure was announced, cannot fail to draw the same inference from the complaints, which, under the opposite system, we have since heard of extra population, and the various schemes we have seen brought forward to provide for those, whose existence we now regret, by grants of money on loan, by encouragement of plans of emigration, and by other means, which it is needless to enumerate.

For it is impossible not to perceive that these complaints of extra population and of extra production originate from the same cause; indeed, the phrases, now so familiar to our ears, were hardly known in our language till the cessation of the war expenditure, and the aggravation of its effects, by the project of forcibly withdrawing part of our revenue from expenditure, to increase our capital at a time when, from the diminution of expenditure, there could be the least natural demand for labour, whether performed by capital, or by the hand of man.

In confirmation of these opinions, the state of other countries might be referred to, where complaints of poverty and want of demand for the productions of industry are as loud as they are with us; a fact which at once negatives the false opinions too prevalent amongst the industrious classes of this country, that their distresses arise from the encouragement given to foreign industry,—and establishes the doctrines that have been here advanced. For there is but one common cause, which can account for the same distress existing in this country and in France, and that is the loss of that great extra expenditure, to which the policy of both countries gave rise for such a length of time, as artificially to create an increase of the hands employed in, as well as of the means of performing, labour, to an extent far greater, than that for which there existed a demand under the ordinary circumstances of either country,—whilst in both the source of calamity is aggravated by the artificial diminution of the natural demand for labour created by abstracting a part of the revenue, which would be expended in the produce of industry, if not, by legislative enactment devoted to accumulation, a policy, in adopting which the people of that country have thought it prudent to follow our example.

I have now, however imperfectly, executed the arduous task imposed upon me by a sense of public duty.

First,—I have stated to you the grounds on which, instead of feeling any inclination to praise the Fourth Report of the Committee of Finance, I am compelled to say that, on examination, it appears to have recommended to Parliament a line of conduct directly opposed to that which must be considered as the result of the principles it laid down.

Secondly,—I have endeavoured to prove to you that the old argument, founded on inferences by analogy from the effect of men's conduct in private life—the only plea for recommending the continuance of a Sinking Fund—on which this Committee has relied, is totally fallacious, and that it must lead those who rest upon it to unwarrantable conclusions.

I have also assigned my reasons for thinking that a Sinking Fund, far from counteracting the sudden variation in the distribution of property, which I have contended is the only evil raising the means of de-fraying extraordinary expenditure by funding inflicts, is the device of all others that tends most to aggravate the mischief.

Lastly,—I have endeavoured to convince you and the public that, when the Committee, in pursuing the old beaten track of reasoning from the analogies of private life, state that, if a nation, on the return of peace, does not make efforts to discharge its past burdens, they must become too great for any people to support, and that the fabric of public credit must crumble under accumulated pressure,—they have delivered opinions completely unfounded; for, in truth, a great extra expenditure, which they regard as impoverishing a community, is the most fertile means of increasing its public wealth; whilst a Sinking Fund, such as they recommend for enriching a community, must always be the most active means of impoverishing it.

Whether my efforts to convince either you or the public of the accuracy and truth of these highly important propositions will be successful, it is not for me to anticipate; but I must confess myself sanguine in my expectation that, if (which I hope will not be the case) this Committee should be called upon to renew their labours, their future Report must show that I have not laboured in vain. Because it would be strange indeed, if the Committee composed of men, many of whom pride themselves on professing and acting on what they call liberal principles, and on their support of what they call a system of free trade, should, after being forced to more mature reflection, continue to recommend a strict adherence to the most severe of all legislative restraints on the use of property and the conduct of trade ; for in that light I must regard a law that regulates, without inquiry and examination, the quantity of the revenue of the country that it would be annually expedient forcibly to withdraw from expenditure, and to convert into capital.

Yours, &c. &c. &c.

LAUDERDALE.

APPENDIX.

APPENDIX.

SKETCH

OF A

PETITION TO PARLIAMENT,

Submitted to the consideration of all who feel for the Welfare of the Country, or for the Distresses of the Lower Orders of the People;

OF WHICH

A FEW COPIES WERE PRIVATELY PRINTED AND CIRCULATED IN 1820.

The humble Petition of   *   *   *   *   *   *
To   *   *   *   *   *   *   *   *   *

SHEWETH,

THAT whilst your Petitioners deeply lament the depressed state of the agriculture, commerce, and manufactures of these kingdoms, and the consequent distress in which the labourers in these several branches are involved, they feel convinced that no relief can be given to any one branch of industry at the expense of another, without increasing the sufferings even of those whose interest it is intended to promote; and that every arrangement which directly benefits any one class of the community, without injury to any other, must indirectly prove advantageous to all.

That your Petitioners, therefore, cannot join in the prayer of any petition, which, imploring freedom of trade in all articles not connected with the public revenue, may be construed into a prayer for keeping up the duties by which manufactures are protected, and repealing the protection afforded by the Legislature to agriculture, as corn is the only article which is protected by regulation.

That, on the same principle, your Petitioners are precluded from co-operating with those, who, in this moment of distress, have very injudiciously petitioned your Honourable House to adopt measures, which they are wrong in thinking would, under all their bearings, relieve the agricultural interest, even if they were right in supposing that they would add to the prices of the necessaries of life.

That your Petitioners, convinced that perfect freedom from restraint is the means best calculated to give the most advantageous direction to the capital and industry of every country, and to secure to it the greatest possible state of prosperity, deeply lament the long-continued existence of that restrictive, protective, and prohibitory system, which has been for ages sanctioned by the legislature of this country.

That nevertheless your Petitioners feel that it is under this system these kingdoms attained an unparalleled state of prosperity ; and as there are many regimens under which the human frame enjoys perfect health, so your Petitioners are convinced that there are many political and commercial arrangements, under which a community may enjoy very great prosperity.

That when they, therefore, reflect how much the restrictive and prohibitory system is connected and interwoven by long habit with every branch of our industry, they must deprecate any hasty and inconsiderate dereliction of these our ancient habits, by hastily adopting a new system of commercial regulations, however much it may be more consonant to the sound principles by which the economical policy of a country ought to be regulated.

For your Petitioners feel it their duty humbly to state to your Honourable House that this, a time of deep distress, does not appear to them to be the moment for indulging in experiments; and must therefore implore your Honourable House to make no alteration in any part of our legislative code, which affects the agriculture, manufactures, or commerce of the country, without a full investigation of the particular case, and an ample consideration of the remote consequences in relation to other branches of industry, which cannot fail to ensue under our artificial and complicated system.

That, convinced as your Petitioners are of the necessity of extreme caution in the alteration of the laws, relative to any particular branch of industry, they nevertheless feel it their duty to implore the attention of your Honourable House to one artificial, legislative restraint, on the natural destination of the property of the country, which they sincerely believe is at this moment equally injurious to every class of the community.

That the general distress now existing, appears to your Petitioners to arise from the low price of commodities, which does not afford sufficient remuneration for the labour of those who are employed in producing them; and as price depends on the proportion between supply and demand, they are convinced your Honourable House must perceive that this evil can only be remedied by an increase of demand for the commodities produced. For your Petitioners humbly conceive that the feelings of humanity, which, in this country, always predominate, must shrink back from the idea of restoring the necessary remunerating value to our commodities by a diminution of supply; an operation that would inevitably occasion the destruction of all that portion of our population employed in the formation of what constitutes the existing extra supply.

That, as the most immediate and effectual means of very greatly increasing the demand for commodities, and consequently the price thereof, your Petitioners humbly request to call the attention of your Honourable House to the salutary effects that would ensue from a suspension of that forced accumulation of capital, which the legislature enacts by persevering, at this moment, in the appropriation of a large portion of our revenue towards a Sinking Fund. For your Honourable House must be fully aware that there is no portion of the funds so appropriated, which is not annually raised by taxation, on a people who have been subjected to an increase of taxes unparalleled in rapidity; and that by persevering in this system of accumulation, you are transferring from the hands of the consumers a portion of their revenues to Commissioners, who are bound by law to employ it as capital, whilst, if it had remained in the hands to whom it naturally belonged, it would have been expended in the purchase of consumable commodities; more particularly at a moment when many of the consumers of the country are deprived of a due supply of the necessaries, and almost all, more or less, of the luxuries which they were accustomed to enjoy.

That, if this practice is persevered in, your Petitioners look forward with dismay to the calamity in which the country must be involved; for, if it is true, which all writers on political economy concur in asserting, that the whole quantity of industry employed to bring any commodity to the market, naturally suits itself to the effectual demand, and constantly aims at bringing the precise quantity thither that is sufficient to supply that demand—it follows that this diminution of demand, forced by our accumulating fund, must occasion a similar diminution of the productions of the country.

That your Petitioners must most seriously conjure your Honourable House calmly and deliberately to reflect on the consequences of the measures you have pursued and are pursuing.

For twenty-four years, ending the beginning of the year 1819, your Honourable House was pleased, on an average, to raise by loan or otherwise, twenty-eight millions of the capital of the country, and to sanction the expenditure thereof to meet the demands of the war in which we were so long engaged.

You have seen that this extra expenditure beyond what the revenue naturally afforded, created a formidable increase in the demand for labour;—that a rise in the value of labour ensued, and that this extended demand—continued for twenty-four years—created, as must have been expected, an increase of population, such as to adjust the supply of labour to the demand for it.

To your Honourable House, therefore, the consequences of a line of conduct directly the reverse must be apparent : for twenty-four years you persisted in annually expending a large portion of the capital of the country as revenue ; you are now by law forcing a large portion of the revenue to be laid out as capital. By the former line of conduct, you inevitably increased the demand for labour, which, augmenting the wages of labour, encouraged the increase of population; by adopting the latter system, you must as inevitably diminish the demand for labour, which, by lowering the wages of labour, must devote to starvation that extra population, which you have thus incautiously created; forcing them, in the mean time, to have recourse for sustenance to the miserable pittance afforded by our wretched system of Poor Laws, which is no less ruinous to the property that still remains to the landholder, than it is prejudicial to the interests of the fair and honest manufacturer, and destructive of the industry and morals of the lower orders of society.

It is on these grounds your Petitioners humbly think it cannot be disputed by any one, who gives a moment's consideration to the subject, that if many of the most oppressive taxes, the produce of which is now applied to this forced accumulation, were repealed, it would contribute to the immediate relief of those who pay them; whilst the expenditure of the funds they are now obliged to deliver over to the commissioners, to be employed as capital, would create such an immediate increase of demand for our commodities in the home market, as, by restoring the due proportion between demand and supply, would greatly contribute towards re-establishing a remunerating price for the labourers of every class of the industrious throughout the community.

That your Petitioners humbly beg leave to state to your Honourable House, that this great and beneficial result may be obtained, without doing injustice to any class of the community; for, your Honourable House will find, on examination, that the institution of the Sinking Fund was a measure adopted by the legislature, on a belief, which many now think erroneous, that it would be generally advantageous for the public interest, and not with a view to benefit any one particular class of the community. And your Honourable House must be convinced that the stockholders can have no right to claim the continued existence of a benefit exclusively advantageous to them, at the expence of the rest of the country, when you reflect that great part of the existing debt was contracted by payments made to the public in currency depreciated from 15 to 28 per cent.:— whilst by legislative enactment you are now about to pay the interest upon the capital so advanced in the standard coin of these realms.

That your Petitioners must humbly repeat to your Honourable House that this is a moment of unprecedented distress, from want of demand for those commodities, on the formation of which the existence of a considerable part of the population of this country depends; they indeed, in conjunction with many others are sanguine that great benefit will be derived from the operation of time, when property becomes permanently fixed in the hands, in which it is placed by the new distribution, to which the enormous expenditure of our war has given rise.

Nevertheless, it appears to your Petitioners, and they trust it will appear to your Honourable House, and to the community at large, highly inexpedient to abstract, at this moment, so important a share of the revenue from expenditure, with a view to accumulate it into capital, for the benefit of posterity, who, it is confidently believed, will exist in times when an increased demand may have relieved the community from that state of distress, in which it is now involved; for your Petitioners are convinced that there is not a Member of your Honourable House, who would not conceive an individual, possessing a revenue capable, during a famine, of purchasing food sufficient to sustain himself and those dependent upon him, to be insane, if he allowed himself and his family to perish, rather than submit to break in upon the sum he was annually in the habit of accumulating for his posterity; yet it is with deep regret your Petitioners perceive that this is the line of conduct that the legislature of this country, bound to protect the public by the same ties that a father is bound to protect his family, is at this moment pursuing.

Your petitioners therefore humbly implore your Honourable House, to take into your immediate consideration the propriety of suspending the operation of the Sinking Fund, by repealing taxes to the amount of the sum appropriated for accumulation; by the judicious performance of which duty your Petitioners are convinced that you will afford great relief to many classes of the lower orders of society, and general advantage to all, resulting from the expenditure of that portion of the revenue now devoted to accumulation, in the purchase of commodities of our produce and manufactures, to which it would naturally be appropriated, if not forcibly converted into capital by legislative interference.